REDESIGN

How to Create Success on Your Own Terms

ANDREA MERICAN

REDESIGN

HOW TO CREATE SUCCESS ON YOUR OWN TERMS

ANDREA MERICAN

For more information: hello@andreamerican.com

ISBN (paperback): 978-1-962280-41-9

ISBN (ebook): 978-1-962280-42-6

A Special Gift Just for You!

Thank you for diving into my book! To show my appreciation, I've created a collection of valuable resources that accompany each chapter designed to help you put the insights you've learned into action.

Use the link below to download all these tools for free:

andreamerican.com/redesignbook

To all those who dare to dream, who persevere through challenges, and who courageously carve their own paths in pursuit of their passions. This book is dedicated to you, the designers of your own destinies. May it inspire and encourage you on your journey to greatness.

Table of Contents

Chapter 1

Journey

Have you ever had a day when you woke up and found yourself questioning what happened? What happened to the body you used to admire? To the face that radiated happiness? To a day full of endless possibilities? To the future you once eagerly anticipated?

I know I have.

We all have dreams of what our life will become. We all nurture hopes and expectations that often do not come true.

What you do next is the pivotal moment.

Do you climb back into bed? Do you sink into depression and dwell in sadness and apathy? Or do you decide it is time for a change and desire something better? Do you believe that better is possible and is already on its way?

That is what I want to share with you. Drawing from my own experiences, I aim to reignite the flame of hope within you and restore your belief in more.

This book is dedicated to anyone who has ever had a dream, only to be told it was unrealistic, crazy, or simply unattainable.

It's for those who dared to pursue their dreams, passions, or entrepreneurial endeavors, but things didn't go as planned.

This book speaks to those who thought that they were too old to start again, it was too late in the game, or time had passed them by.

I am confident that every trial, hardship, and lesson learned along my journey, which I now share with you, was worthwhile if I can:

- Help just one person realize a long-held dream
- Give one person the courage to get back up and try again
- Empower one person to take that next pivotal step toward their true desires
- Inspire one person to break free from others' expectations and pursue their unique path
- Motivate one person to transform their challenges into opportunities for growth and success

By the time you finish reading this book, you will:

- Be encouraged that wherever you are right now is precisely where you are meant to be
- Be inspired by my journey—from being a poor kid living in a single-wide mobile home, an art school dropout, and a minimum-wage earner to becoming a successful entrepreneur who travels the world with her husband and enjoys both time freedom and financial freedom

- Be assured that you can reach your goals too
- Be aware that your mindset, goals, habits, and discipline can pave the way to any destination you envision for your life
- Be confident you have what it takes inside you to fulfill your dreams

By following the step-by-step action plans outlined in these pages and in my book resources, you can not only achieve but surpass anything you set your mind to.

As a business coach and consultant, nothing brings me greater joy than assisting entrepreneurs in building, expanding, and scaling their businesses. I love meeting with people who are full of excitement and ideas, then guiding them to develop their dreams and visions into something tangible.

One of my superpowers is breaking chaos down into simple steps. These small steps are how businesses are developed. I want to share the lessons I've learned, the hurdles I've overcome, and the shortcuts I've created to help others on their entrepreneurial journeys.

My goal is for you, the reader, to learn from my trials and triumphs, my failures and successes, my decades-long journey, and the habits I've cultivated to take a quantum leap into your own success story. Whether you are an entrepreneur or not, these strategies and tools will help you design a life you love.

My Story

In a recent conversation with my husband, I found myself reminiscing about my early twenties, when I was working for minimum wage in retail. Soon after, I got my first administrative position and earned slightly more hourly. I vividly recall believing that this was going to be my life. I would get a job as an administrative assistant in some company, earn my hourly wage, work in a cubicle, hopefully get married, and live my life.

Fast-forward twenty-four years, and I scarcely recognize the woman I was then.

I have been an entrepreneur since I was eighteen and built a thriving Internet business in the early 2000s. I have been instrumental in establishing multiple high-income-generating real estate investment companies from the ground up, supporting visionaries and dreamers in realizing their ambitions. I have made a business out of creating art and painting beautiful watercolor paintings over the last twelve years. My husband and I have invested in rental properties, benefiting from the residual income they afford us each month. I have been a successful real estate broker in Arizona for seventeen years. I currently coach and consult for entrepreneurs, small business owners, and real estate agents while enjoying time freedom and traveling the world with my husband. My life looks like a fairy tale compared to the limited life I envisioned in my early twenties.

Reflecting on my journey, I asked myself what differentiated my path from someone else's story. Was it simply a matter of belief? Did

I experience a breakthrough, believing I could have more? Or was it the culmination of countless books, classes, seminars, podcasts, and conversations over decades that increased my belief in what was possible and helped me take risks, try new things, and put myself out there in ways I never thought possible?

This book encapsulates much of that story, from lack to abundance. It explores the mindset, goals, habits, time management skills, productivity hacks, and leaps of faith that made me into the entrepreneur I am today. Even more exciting is the realization, after many years, that I am able to share this journey with you.

If my experiences, insights, and lessons helped me go from a college dropout making minimum wage to a successful entrepreneur enjoying time freedom, what if I could help another person do that? What if I could help just one other person fulfill their dream? Wouldn't that be an honor and a privilege?

So that is where this book began. I have documented all the mentors, teachers, and life lessons that have built me. If one, two, or even five of those lessons or tools resonate with you and help you grow and develop the fantastic business or create the amazing life you've only dreamed of, then I have achieved my purpose.

At the end of each chapter, you'll find two sections designed to help you take action. The first is "Books That Changed My Life." Over the years, I have read countless books, many of which have been truly transformational. I've included the most powerful ones at the end of each chapter, along with a complete list in the book resources.

The most important section is the "Chapter Action Steps and Resources." Here you'll find valuable tools I created specifically for you to implement the lessons and strategies outlined in each chapter, which can all be downloaded in the book resources link below:

andreamerican.com/redesignbook

Chapter 2
Mindset

I'm not sure when I first heard the word *mindset* or if I even understood what it meant. But I am certainly very aware of it now.

I grew up in a pessimistic home with a family that waited for the other shoe to drop. It was assumed that life is hard and we should not expect too much from it or other people. Of course, I wasn't aware anyone lived differently. I thought it was normal for people to complain and worry about life. My single mother was gripped by fear and anxiety, as if she was waiting for the next bad thing to happen. We lived simply and on very little money, but life was okay.

When I was a little girl, I dreamed that things would be different someday. While I lay in bed at night, I played a game. I closed my eyes and dreamed of living in a big, beautiful house with lovely furniture. I walked through each room and each perfect setting in my mind, picturing all the beautiful things there. In the daytime, I would stare out my bedroom window and imagine I was a princess in a castle and thought of all the lovely things I would have.

But I was a pragmatic kid. I didn't actually believe in the fairy tale, although my heart longed for it. I didn't think any of it would ever be real. No adult ever told me I could be anything I wanted. They never told me my dreams would come true. They just told me to work hard in school and get good grades. They told me to get a stable government job so I would have good benefits. They might even have told me to marry well.

I did earn excellent grades and was a top student. But I didn't want a conventional life. I wanted to attend art school and become an artist. My high school guidance counselor told me that was stupid and that I should become a doctor or lawyer. I didn't listen to her. I followed my dream and went to art school. I also ignored my family's advice to get a government job, knowing that sitting in a cubicle all day wasn't for me. I married well because my husband is amazing, though he didn't have any money either. So I probably disappointed some well-meaning people who gave me that advice.

It wasn't until 2008 that I became aware of the concept of mindset. The CEO looked at me in a meeting one day as I was shooting down someone's idea and said, "Andrea, why do you have to be so negative?"

I was taken aback. I'd always thought of myself as a happy person. *Do people think I'm negative?* I wondered.

It turns out that to entrepreneurs and dreamers, I did come across as negative. I was so used to shoving my dreams to the back burner, waiting for the other shoe to drop, and anticipating the worst-case scenario that I didn't allow exciting new ideas, what-if-it's-possible dreams, or even true hope to enter my mind.

This startling experience led me on a discovery mission. I read books by Dr. Wayne Dyer, Eckhart Tolle, Don Miguel Ruiz, Tim Ferriss, and others. I attended seminars and workshops. I learned phrases like "Thoughts are things." I was shocked at the amount of information available on how our minds work and affect our lives. I'd had no idea that over my three decades of negative thinking, I'd been carving out neural pathways in my brain. I was astonished to learn that this behavior could be changed. Indeed, it can!

I have spent the last sixteen years learning to rewire my brain for the positive, the possible, and the hopeful. I wouldn't say it was easy, but it was essential. Today, I am vigilant about what I allow into my thoughts. I had to start by making choices that helped guard my mind, like not watching or reading the news daily, choosing what kind of TV and movies I watched, and even what music I listened to. I had to remove a few toxic people from my life because they were not healthy for me. I also had to become very self-aware. It is virtually impossible to prevent negative thoughts from popping into your brain. Believe me, I've tried. I had to learn that it's okay if a thought presents itself but that I don't have to buy into it. Thoughts will come and go, but it is up to me to believe it, act on it, or dismiss it.

My husband used to get upset about emails that didn't matter. One day, he asked me, "What do I do about this email? How am I supposed to respond?"

I walked over to his computer and hit the Delete key. Some emails don't require a response. Same with thoughts. Sometimes, you just need to delete them and move on with your day without worrying about where the thought came from, how you need to deal with it, or what happens if the thought comes up again. Just delete.

Self-Awareness

Self-awareness is another concept I learned along this mindset journey. What is self-awareness, and why does it matter?

Becoming self-aware is a starting point for self-improvement. By getting to know your thoughts, feelings, strengths, and weaknesses, you can discover why you behave the way you do and how those actions affect your life and those around you. The best part is that understanding yourself and being more aware gives you the freedom to create the life you want by creating positive change.

The first step to self-awareness is listening to your thoughts. Pay attention when you feel bad. Pause for a moment to see if there is a thought behind that feeling, then identify it.

The next step is paying attention to your words. Are you complaining all the time? Are you telling other people about all your troubles and worries? Are you verbally assuming the worst-case scenario? Dive into this and find out why. Where are these words coming from? What thoughts lit the flame of this complaint fest you're in right now?

The third step is more involved, but it is essential to your growth in this area. Set aside some time for just you and your thoughts. Bring a journal and pen. Now that you've become more aware of your words and thoughts, find out where they are coming from. What are the limiting beliefs behind them that are calling the shots in your life? You may not even be aware of them. You need to discover the lies you tell yourself—the lies you live by.

My Five Self-Limiting Beliefs

I'll be very vulnerable here and share some of the lies I have lived with and had to overcome.

Lie #1: I don't feel beautiful.

Lie #2: I am not good enough.

Lie #3: I am not worth that much money.

Lie #4: I'll never make a good, full-time living as an entrepreneur.

Lie #5: Money is hard to come by.

It's difficult to reflect on all these false beliefs I carried around for years. However, the exciting news is that each one of us has the power to rewrite these lies into empowering truths that can transform your mindset and your results.

Follow the formula below and use the worksheet in your book resources to work through this activity in your own life.

Lie #1: I don't feel beautiful.

The truth: Whenever I post a photo online, everyone says I am beautiful. My husband thinks I am the most beautiful woman on the planet. My friends tell me that I am lovely. My inner character is what matters—and God says that is beautiful.

My new belief: I am beautiful inside and out.

Lie #2: I am not good enough.

Truth: I am *more* than good. I am amazing. I am talented. I am kind. I am intelligent. I am a unicorn.

My new belief: I show up with excellence. I give my very best every day, and that is more than good. I am exceptional.

Lie #3: I am not worth that much money.

Truth: Correct. I am worth *more* money. I am capable of delivering CEO-level business-building skills to any business. I am clearly worth $250,000, $500,000, and much more. My life experience is valuable to the right people.

My new belief: I am worth a seven-figure income.

Lie #4: I'll never make a good, full-time living from my own business.

Truth: This is a lie my parents, teachers, and society told me. Many successful entrepreneurs make a full-time living from their creative pursuits. I will make as much money as I desire if I do what I was born to do; inject my passion, heart, and soul into the work every day; and give to people what they cannot give themselves.

My new belief: I love what I do, and I get paid well for it.

Lie #5: Money is hard to come by.

Truth: I remember when I used to wake up, jump out of bed, run to my computer, and count thousands of dollars in my inbox! I remember when I woke up and discovered I sold a painting online. I remember when I sold out another coaching program!

My new belief: Money comes to me effortlessly.

I shared these real-life limiting beliefs that I had to overcome so you'd see the steps you'll want to follow to remove those empty lies that are running your life.

Your homework is to set aside some time for just you and your journal, and write down all the lies you are living by. All the ugly beliefs that have haunted you for years. Write them all down, no matter how they sound, without judgment. This is only for you.

Once you have all those lies staring you in the face, write down the truth. Think of all you have accomplished. Think of how loved you are. Think of the hardships you have overcome. Think of how kind and good and lovely you are deep down inside. Write out those truths. Feel them, believe them, and declare them out loud.

Then, write a new belief for each old lie. Tape those new beliefs to your mirror, wall, refrigerator, or wherever you want. The old lies are gone. Your new life is already on its way!

By going through this practice in a deep and meaningful way, feeling those new truths you wrote down, and reminding yourself of them on a daily basis, you will crack open a window into a new world that is waiting for you beyond the lies that have been keeping you from your true purpose.

> "Your beliefs become your thoughts,
> Your thoughts become your words,
> Your words become your actions,
> Your actions become your habits,
> Your habits become your values,
> Your values become your destiny."

— Gandhi

Reticular Activating System (Thoughts Are Things!)

Have you ever heard the phrase, "Thoughts are things"? It comes from a quote by Napoleon Hill: "Thoughts are things," and powerful things when mixed with definiteness of purpose, persistence, and a burning desire . . ."[1]

When you dig into this idea that the things you think about, especially the ones you think about repeatedly, come to fruition, it will rock

---

1. "Thoughts are things." the Napoleon Hil Foundation, June 27, 2019, https://www.naphill.org/tftd/thought-for-the-day-june-27-2019/.

your world. If you are a negative thinker, it will shake you to your core. Someone once said that everything you are experiencing right now results from how you have been thinking over a long period of time. Try telling that to an unhappy person. You'll get an earful of angry, retaliatory words thrown back at you. They can't believe that their current state of being broke, unhappy, lonely, angry, or miserable could possibly be because of anything they have thought. But it is true. Just take the reticular activating system as an example.

The *Textbook of Clinical Neurology* says, "The reticular activating system (RAS) is a network of neurons located in the brain stem that project anteriorly to the hypothalamus to mediate behavior, as well as both posteriorly to the thalamus and directly to the cortex for activation of awake, desynchronized cortical EEG patterns."[2]

What does that mean?

You know when you are deciding to buy a new car? You've always dreamed of having a Model S Tesla long-range four-door red sedan. You have never driven one, and you don't know anyone who has one. But you've seen it online or on TV, and you think, *That is my dream car.* What happens next is the reticular activating system. You start seeing red Model S Teslas *everywhere!* You can't drive to work without seeing one. You can't go on the freeway without seeing one. You can't park in a shopping center without seeing one.

That is your RAS at work. The more you think about something over and over, the more it starts appearing in your life. Whether

---

2. Michael J. Aminoff et al., *Textbook of Clinical Neurology*, 3rd ed. (Amsterdam, The Netherlands: Elsevier Inc., 2007): 1319–1364.

those thoughts are positive or negative, it doesn't matter. They will still show up.

The great news is you can learn to use this to your advantage.

Visualize your life the way you want it to be. Start dwelling on all the possibilities, hopes, and dreams you want. Close your eyes and see yourself running your dream business. Imagine earning the income you've always wanted. Close your eyes and see yourself looking fabulous, healthy, and fit. Imagine yourself curled up on the couch in your dream house with the love of your life. This will jump-start your RAS. If you practice it daily, you'll experience more opportunities for these good and positive things to show up. You will be able to increase your belief that what you are working toward is already on its way to you.

Let's face it: life is difficult, and being an entrepreneur is even more challenging. We get let down, disappointed, rejected, and sometimes kicked in the gut. There must be a way to get back up and not become derailed when the going gets tough. Thoughts become things, and that is the truth. That is why keeping your mind right at all times is crucial, especially when building or growing a business.

Seeds or Weeds

Are you planting seeds or weeds in your mind each day?

As an amateur gardener, I can correlate things we plant in the soil and what they grow into with the seeds we plant in our minds. You can view actions, thoughts, and intentions as positive or negative—either seeds or weeds. If you want a life filled with joy, compassion, and fulfillment, sow seeds of kindness, empathy, and gratitude. Being mindful of which kind of fruit you are sowing is vital. As any gardener knows, it is too easy for weeds (negative thoughts) to choke out healthy plants (positive thoughts) from cultivating good in our minds and lives.

Negative Bias

If we know all this great information about mindset and its importance to our lives, why is it so hard to remain positive and ensure we are planting seeds and not weeds? Do you ever wonder why it is so difficult to stay positive? Or why is it so easy to hear, "You need to think positively," while negative thoughts keep coming into your head? There is a scientific reason for it. Humans have a negativity bias.[3]

The interesting thing about negative thinking is that once your mind starts on this path, the number of negative thoughts rapidly increases. I have watched it in my own life. If I allow myself to complain about something one day, the next day, I will inevitably complain about more things, and the following day, even more. Soon, weeks will go by, and my overall attitude will be more cynical and my words harsher. If you are not aware that you are allowing this to happen, it can spiral downward to the point where it affects your mental health and your relationships with others.

---

3. Kendra Cherry, "What Is the Negativity Bias?" VeryWellMind, updated November 13, 2023, https://www.verywellmind.com/negative-bias-4589618.

Let's be honest: no one wants to be around someone who constantly complains or looks at everything negatively. It's depressing. The world is full of problems, and we each carry our own burdens. We definitely don't need to add other people's laundry list of complaints to our day.

When I see myself going down this path of negativity, I turn it around by being mindful of it and watching my words. Sometimes, I can't catch a thought, but I can usually hear my words and whether they are positive or negative. Finally, I choose gratitude. When I look at my life and count my tremendous list of blessings, I can't help but be grateful.

Gratitude is the antidote to negativity.

Words, Words, Words

If our thoughts create things, our words create worlds. If you go through your day speaking negatively, complaining, and talking about all the bad things in your life, guess what? You'll get more of all those things you say you hate. Every time you speak words of complaint and anger and say, "It's not fair," or, "I can't stand this," and "Life sucks," you just bring all those words to reality. You create a world with your words.

I have seen this with several people, which is sad to watch. The more they whine and complain about how bad life is, the more they keep spiraling downward until everything in their reality is that bad.

So, how do you turn this around? Or better yet, how do you prevent it from happening?

Here's a tool that works and is fun: do the opposite. If you are experiencing all things bad in your world, replace your negative speech with positive for things to improve. Seek out the good every single day.

Did you wake up alive? That's the first good.

Did you have the good fortune to make a lovely cup of coffee in your own home? That's the second good.

Are you building your own business? That's the third.

Did you watch someone walk a dog down the street and see how he wagged his tail and did that doggy smiling face? That's the fourth.

You must intentionally look for good in life.

Once you start seeing the good in your day, think about the good things in your life. Are you healthy? Be grateful for that gift. Does someone in the world love and care about you? Be grateful for that person. Did a stranger smile at you at the grocery store? Smile back at them and be grateful for their kindness.

Now that you are seeing good and thinking good thoughts, you can start speaking good things into your life. When you are driving to a meeting all by yourself, say out loud, "I'm so happy and grateful for this beautiful day!" Or say, "I'm so thankful that I run a thriving business so I can pay all my bills." Tell someone they look nice today. Thank someone, mean it, and be sincere.

These are all just small steps that will lead to more good flooding into your life. It might feel awkward at first, but I encourage you to do it anyway. It takes time to create a new habit. Just think about how long it took to develop the bad habit of seeing everything in the world as bad and out to get you. Now, you are training your brain to overcome that and see that the world is amazing and beautiful and has a place for you.

Repetition and intentionality are key. Just keep going every day, and you'll find you're creating a more positive world you can enjoy and be grateful for.

Gratitude Practice

Do you have a daily gratitude practice? If not, you are missing out on one of the easiest ways to rewire your brain for positivity. Adding this practice to your life is very simple and doesn't have to take up a lot of time. You can do this in several ways. Just pick the method that resonates with you the most.

- **Gratitude as a part of your morning quiet time**. I incorporate gratitude into my daily prayer time. It is my favorite part of prayer because I get this huge smile just thinking about all the blessings in my life, and I get to pause and thank God for each one. This is an amazing way to start my day.
- **A gratitude journal**. Some people like to keep a journal by their bed. Before they go to sleep, they write down everything they were grateful for during the day. This is a beautiful practice because it trains your brain to intentionally

look for different ways to be thankful. You may be grateful because someone held the door for you or told you that you looked lovely. You may be thankful because you got a new client. You may be grateful because you missed a car accident by inches this afternoon. You may be thankful that you have supportive friends. The possibilities are endless when you are on the lookout for ways to be grateful.

- **A gratitude dinner practice**. This is perfect for families. Be intentional about eating dinner together every night. No phones or technology allowed. As you eat your meal together, go around the table and ask each person what they were grateful for that day. This is a healthy way to stay connected and share quality time while incorporating an effective mindfulness practice.

Pick a practice that sounds best to you, then use it consistently for three weeks. Watch your thoughts change from negative to positive right before your eyes.

Attachment

The Buddhists say that attachment is the cause of all suffering.[4]

I agree with this truth. I can be attached to a person and how I feel they should respond, speak to me, or act around me. When they

---

4. Janelle Renée, "Desire Is as Desire Does: A Path of Suffering or a Path Towards Enlightenment," Cal State East Bay, csueastbay.edu, accessed May 16, 2024, https://www.csueastbay.edu/philosophy/reflections/2011-2012/contents/jane-rene.html#:~:text=At%20the%20heart%20of%20this,path%20to%20liberation%20from%20suffering.

don't behave as I think they should, I may feel hurt, upset, or let down. I can also be attached to a goal. I define my goal, set it, and work hard to bring it to fruition. When it does not happen how or when I think it should, I feel defeated and upset, like I have failed.

I am attached to expectations.

This one gets me all the time. I expect an event, or even a day, to go a certain way. I think this or that will happen, and then nothing goes as planned. Something goes wrong, or everything goes wrong. It derails my whole day! I feel angry. I feel sad. I feel a variety of negative emotions. As the Buddhists say, I am suffering all because I had all these expectations in place and was attached to a specific outcome.

Now, the true question is, How do we live without attachments?

Of course, we can't use *attached* as an all-encompassing term. We are attached to our spouses, partners, jobs, children, families, etc. That is not the attachment I am referring to. I am talking about being attached to how things should be, according to *me*.

If I am attached to my way, expectations, and exact plans, I will continually be let down. I must find a way to plan and set goals but hold them loosely, as in allowing the universe or life to alter things for something better to happen.

Spontaneity is a beautiful thing. Freedom is a wonderful feeling. Being tied down, trapped, and chained to my ways is not living.

Shift in Mindset

In the summer of 2020, we were about five months deep in the COVID-19 pandemic. I was just fine for about the first three months. Don't get me wrong, I was still experiencing anxiety and fear, and I read the news every single day, which got me more worked up. But overall, my mindset was still pretty good. We had a ton of house projects going, I launched a new painting series, I was able to work on tasks I'd wanted to do forever, and I had more time to sit and talk with my husband, Paul, and listen to music together. I told him I thought this time was a gift. Everyone complains about not having enough time and being too busy. Well, people, here you go!

In June 2020, I wrote new goals, started a gratitude practice, and read three great nonfiction books to motivate and propel me forward. I focused on eating well, exercising, and being healthy.

Even so, it was a month full of challenges to work through. I was in the middle of tenant issues, property manager problems, and a refinance from hell. In Arizona, our COVID-19 numbers started spiking; we were on the national news for being the new hot spot. Just as we finally felt comfortable going to a restaurant for dinner, we were on lockdown again. I started feeling depressed. And I never feel depressed. Happiness and energy are my natural emotions, not depression. I started asking what the point of anything was.

Why do I need to work on my business? I wondered. *Why do I need to paint or create art? Who cares anyway? What is the point?*

Nothing mattered. It felt like something inside me died.

After a few months of this roller coaster of emotions, I realized I'd let my mindset go to a very negative place. It was time to figure this out. I wanted to know when we would get out of the dark days of the pandemic. I asked, How can we rise above this? I wanted to be happy again. I wanted to be motivated. I wanted to set goals and achieve them and then celebrate those achievements! I wanted to really *live* again—and to live a life that mattered.

It was time to shift my perspective. I asked myself, *Why can't I make 2020 one of the best years of my life?* While everyone else wrote it off as the worst year ever, we still had six months left. I decided I could make it unforgettable. I could choose to improve my health, relationships, financial position, and spiritual life. I could learn, grow, and change regardless of the pandemic going on around me.

So I chose to shift my mindset that day. I set a new course and pointed my sails toward a broad reach. I knew I might have to decide to do this every day on the bad days. But making that decision changed everything.

It empowered me. I traveled despite pandemic restrictions and made the most of every trip. I leaned into eating healthy and exercising more. I spent time working on our investment business and exited the company I was working for, taking the entire next year off. I started writing this book because I wanted to share all the lessons I'd learned and the tools and strategies I'd developed to allow me to live my most successful life.

Each of us can choose to focus on things above, what matters, and the big picture. Or we can choose to focus on earthly things, cultural things, or other catastrophes. We can choose to obsess and roll around in our day-to-day miseries. Or we can rise above, set our course, and follow the path to better things, freedom, and where we know we are supposed to go.

Make Life Fun

Another way to shift your mindset is to make life fun. If you find yourself struggling to find positivity in your day, put on some upbeat music. Jump around and sing and dance and play. I'll rock out in my car and sing at the top of my lungs, and I don't care if people in other cars think I'm crazy. I'm having fun.

Add a little spontaneity to your week. Go for an unplanned hike, walk, bike ride, or drive to a place out in nature. Bring a friend or spouse or a dog. Appreciate that you have air to breathe, legs to walk, and eyes to see the beauty around you. Ask a friend or loved one to lunch unexpectedly. Put on your favorite movie, make popcorn, and curl up with a blanket on the couch just because you can. Go shopping for a small gift for yourself or someone you love. Do things you don't usually do that make life more fun.

Perspective

We can all find something to be thankful for in our day. If you try hard, you can even find a positive shift in the mundane or challenging areas of life. I have an amazing friend named Mark. When I tell him a story about getting lost on a trip, being stuck in an airport on a seven-hour delay, or any challenging issue I'm complaining about, he always turns it around by exclaiming, "It's an adventure!" The first few times he did this, I was not amused. But over the years, it has become a funny little way of looking at life, and it does turn my attitude around much faster than if I chose to wallow in the negativity of the situation.

I Like Life

This may sound ridiculous, but hear me out. In order to have a full, rich, rewarding experience in this world, you need to like life. If you keep saying, "I hate life," or "Everything is against me," or "Life is so hard," that is exactly what you're going to get. You'll keep hating life, and life will keep hating you right back.

But if you look for the positive, seek beauty, joy, and fun, and enjoy living, you'll experience a different world. You'll marvel at the colors of the sunset. You'll delight in the laughter of the kids playing on your street. You'll say thank you and smile when someone holds the door open for you. When you like life, every day becomes a chance to appreciate the goodness and blessings around you.

What if you expected good things to come your way? What if you knew in your heart that everything would work out for the best? What if you genuinely and honestly believed that life was for you and not against you?

I'll bet your outlook would be drastically different.

What Is Your Story?

What story are you telling yourself each and every day? Are you telling the story of you being healthy, happy, successful, and loved? Or are you telling the story of you being alone, miserable, and broke? Life will match up to your expectations. I choose to expect only good and wonderful things to come to me.

I choose to tell the story of my life like this:

My spiritual life is full and abundant.

I am a loving, loyal, and fun wife.

I am attracting health, vitality, and fitness to every cell in my body.

I am a successful business coach and consultant.

Money comes to me effortlessly.

I have both time freedom and financial freedom.

I love sharing my gift of art with others.

I take wonderful trips all over the world and the country.

Our friends are amazing, interesting, and outwardly giving.

I inspire and encourage others to live purposeful lives.

My story reminds me how blessed I am and how more blessings are coming my way. My story fills me and fuels me when I read it every morning.

Forgive the past and allow yourself to write the story of your life exactly as you want it to be. Hold fast to those positive, loving, abundant thoughts, and don't allow your old negativity to wedge in there. Show up every morning ready to read your story, then do the work to live it out every day.

Believe that your story is coming true even right now as you write it, and you'll experience life in a whole new way.

Books That Changed My Life

The Power of Intention: Learning to Co-create Your World Your Way by Dr. Wayne Dyer

The Four Agreements: A Practical Guide to Personal Freedom by Don Miguel Ruiz

Mindset: The New Psychology of Success by Carol S. Dweck, PhD

Chapter 2 Action Steps and Resources

Self-limiting beliefs worksheet

Mindset journal prompts

Chapter 3

Values

Now that you have discovered the transformative power of mindset, it's important to recognize the foundational role your core values play in shaping your life. While a positive mindset fuels our journey and gives us the strength to write and live out our personal stories, our values serve as the compass that directs our path. Your values will act as your guiding principles, helping you navigate opportunities and challenges with clarity and conviction.

It has become a popular trend for companies to develop core values. Zappos.com, the popular online shoe company, has these ten core values[5]:

Deliver WOW Through Service

Embrace and Drive Change

Create Fun and a Little Weirdness

Be Adventurous, Creative, and Open-Minded

Pursue Growth and Learning

Build Open and Honest Relationships with Communication

Build a Positive Team and Family Spirit

Do More with Less

Be Passionate and Determined

Be Humble

Nike has a mission statement[6]:

"Our mission is, To bring inspiration and **innovation** to every athlete* in the world. *If you have a body, you are an athlete."

Amazon has a list of Leadership Principles, some of which are[7]:

Ownership

Invent and Simplify

Learn and Be Curious

Deliver Results

---

6. "What Is Nike's Mission?" Nike.org, accessed May 16, 2024, https://www.com/help/a/nikeinc-mission.

7. "Leadership Principles," Amazon.jobs, accessed May 16, 2024, https://www.amazon.jobs/en/principles.

My husband and I were discussing finances the other day, and he said something that resonated with me: "Sure, I can buy you an expensive convertible sports car, and you can drive around to show everyone you're my hot wife, but that doesn't align with our values."

If you or your family do not outline a set of values you live by, you can be easily swayed by things that do not align with what matters to you. A set of values or principles or even a mission or vision statement for your life is incredibly powerful. It helps you weigh decisions more easily and provides a reference point that guides you through the gray areas of life.

How Do You Develop Your Own Personal Values?

What are your personal values? Have you taken the time to write them down? They don't have to be elaborate or detailed, but they must genuinely reflect who you are and how you want to live.

This will come into play when you are faced with difficult decisions. You can weigh the pros and cons and sometimes still not be sure what to do. But if an option doesn't align 100 percent with your list of values, then it is a clear no.

Here is an easy exercise to get you started. Think of the person you admire most. Get clear on who you think they are, what their character is, and how you think they behave when no one else is looking. Write down that person's qualities. Just brainstorm. Don't judge anything you write.

Are they a positive person? Are they honest? Are they physically fit? Are they kind? Do they give generously? Do they help others? Think of everything, and write it down. Next, group the words into categories. One word that could describe several things you wrote could be *health*. One could be *faith*. One phrase could be *loving others*.

Once you have written out the list of qualities and grouped them into categories, it becomes a list of values. These are the values that you appreciate in the person you admire. Since these values are what you admire most in your ideal person, they are likely the same values you want to represent your own life.

Take some time to look over these words or phrases and select five to seven values that you want to embody. Write these down as your personal values. Your list of values will be unique to you, so you may have one-word descriptions or longer phrases or sentences that resonate with you.

Finally, once you have this written list of values, stick them to your wall for a week. See if you feel strongly about them. If you need to add or subtract, adjust as needed.

Your core values may change over time. You may become a parent, or you may become a spouse. You may fall in love with health and fitness. Make alterations if a significant life event calls you to do so. But for the most part, stay true to these values, as they are your guides.

Value Examples

When I did this exercise, I wrote down the things I admired about my ideal person and created this list:

- Faith
- Love and kindness
- Health
- Excellence
- Growth
- Art and creativity
- Honesty and integrity
- Grace
- Financial freedom
- Servant leadership
- Choosing positivity
- Inspires others
- Encourages others

Then, I narrowed it down to a few values I can focus on for me and my life.

My values are:

- Faith
- Health
- Love and kindness

43

- Creativity and growth
- Time freedom and financial freedom
- Excellence

I'll break these down so you can see why I chose them and why they matter to me.

Faith

If I didn't have God in my life, I wouldn't be who I am or think the way I do. My faith is a significant value that runs through every area of my life. It is a core value that anchors the rest of them.

Health

I didn't value health for my first twenty-five years because I was naturally thin. And, of course, I was young. As you age, you realize that good health is a gift, and you better treasure it as long as possible. I value healthy foods, water, and the ability to move my body more than ever. Mental and emotional health matter more to me now too. This value helps me make good daily decisions and build and maintain good habits.

Love and Kindness

As I grow older, I value these more every day. It costs nothing to be kind to another person, yet it is invaluable. I try to give myself grace when I make mistakes and extend this to others. I try to look at the heart of a person's intentions rather than the outward action that may have hurt me. I don't always succeed, but by valuing love and kindness, I try again each day to treat others how I would like to be treated.

Creativity and Growth

You may think I chose creativity because I'm an artist, but it shows up in other areas of my life as well. Being creative means being a problem solver. And I look at life differently than other people. I think outside the box, and I embrace change. In my coaching and consulting business, I use creativity to think of new ways to help a client solve a problem. I use creativity in finances to find new ways to build wealth. My unconventional life is a picture of creativity.

Time Freedom and Financial Freedom

I have valued being financially free for decades now. Once I realized I am not wired to sit in a cubicle and ask for days off, I decided I would have to be self-employed and have zero debt in order to live the life I was meant to live. This value shapes how I spend my money, how I invest, how many possessions I own, the charities I support, and many other areas of my life. Time freedom goes hand in hand with financial freedom for me. I want to be able to wake up when I choose to, structure my day as I please, and travel the world with my husband on our schedule.

Excellence

Excellence: noun; the quality of being outstanding or extremely good.[8]

I love that word. I live by it. If you are going to do something, I believe you should do it right the first time. I use excellence in how I conduct my business. I want to show up on time, prepared, and with

---

8. "Keyword: Excellence," keywords project, Jesus College – University of Cambridge, accessed May 23, 2024, http://keywords.pitt.edu/keywords_defined/excellence.html.

excellent solutions for my client's business challenges. I want to keep my word and always follow through on my commitments. I want to provide quality services no matter what business I am running, whether it's art, consulting, or real estate.

Creating Family Values

I learned this concept from Rachel Hollis. I never thought about discussing values with my husband, but what an amazing idea! If you have kids, there is even more reason. The family should have a set of values that everyone lives by. This makes decisions easier to make and stops arguments in their tracks.

If you have never taken the time to create your personal list of values, I encourage you to consider doing it. Just choose three to five, even up to seven, values that are important to you. Share them with your partner or spouse. Come up with a shared list that you can both connect on. Knowing what the other person holds dear will help you understand them and their motivations in a deeper way.

Why Do Values Matter?

Having personal values that you live by influences how you make decisions—financial decisions, health decisions, social decisions, and personal decisions. They influence how you are relationally in marriage, parenting, and friendships. They guide how you approach your work and business life.

For entrepreneurs, personal values flow through to our businesses. How much more powerful is client and customer acquisition and retention when they connect with your values and experience them through your marketing, services, and products?

Values are very important for a leader. Shared values can connect, unite, and energize others. Think of them as the guiding principles of your life. They're the characteristics and behaviors that motivate you.

Life Audit

Once you have established your values, a life audit is a wonderful way to examine your life and see if it is going in the direction of your values. Once a year, I carve out a few uninterrupted hours to do this.

My favorite method is to open my Apple calendar on my MacBook Pro. I have been keeping this calendar for fifteen years, so I have a ton of data. If it is the end of the year, I go back to January 1 and just start reading through my life as captured on the calendar, week by week. I keep a notebook handy to jot down anything that jumps out to me.

Several years ago, when I performed this life audit, I realized that the business I was involved in at the time was not serving me and my life. While I liked building this business with the visionary of this company, I saw plainly on the screen that my time was filled with meaningless tasks, like interviewing people, hiring them, and training them, just to watch them quit a few months later. Building systems and processes that no one was following was disheartening. It seemed like my days were filled with work that didn't create a real impact or use my true talents.

When you perform your life audit, you may find that you made appointments you didn't want to keep. That you gave your precious time to things that didn't matter to you out of guilt or duty. You may also see that you spend too many hours on work, chores, and unpleasant tasks but not enough hours on love, friends, family, and things that align with your values.

That was a major realization for me. I discovered that my heart wanted to serve, give back, and share with other people, but the majority of my time was spent working in a business that didn't resonate with any of that. It was a real eye-opener. When I was able, I exited that company on good terms. And when I freed up this space, I discovered my love for teaching, coaching, and sharing with others all that I had learned.

I want people to feel encouraged to pursue their dreams and know that there is hope for something better. That is my goal with my business and my life. How can I serve others? How can I share my experiences to save someone time, money, or frustration? How can I teach, coach, or simply inspire another person? Those are things that align with my values. Pursuing a career that makes me feel like I'm giving back to others adds meaning and purpose to my life.

Living in Alignment

Values are a part of us, whether we have named them or not. Discovering what your values are and what you stand for allows you to name your unique, individual approach to life. When you live in a manner that's consistent with your values, you feel like your authentic and true self. You feel personal fulfillment. When you don't live according to your personal values, you feel out of alignment and out of integrity with your true self.

Books That Changed My Life

Siddhartha by Hermann Hesse

Chapter 3 Action Steps and Resources

Life audit

Values worksheet

Chapter 4

Purpose

Identifying and living in alignment with your values is key to feeling authentic and fulfilled. Understanding your purpose builds on the foundation of your values, giving direction to your actions and decisions. By connecting your values with your purpose, you can lead a life that not only feels true to who you are but also resonates with a sense of meaning and direction.

What is your purpose?

This daunting question dangles over all of our heads today. It is asked online, in books, in school, and maybe even on job applications.

What were you put on Earth for?

What is your passion?

What are you uniquely gifted to do?

Some of us were lucky enough to know the answer to this question as children.

My earliest memory of creating art dates back to when I was three years old. My mom gave me a huge chalkboard, attaching pegboard legs so it could be easily moved around the house. Wherever I wanted to draw that day, the chalkboard followed. One treasured photo captures me sitting and smiling beside my chalkboard, proudly pointing to my latest creation. "Look, Mommy, a duck!" I exclaimed. My mom thought my drawing resembled a duck, so she snapped the picture to capture the moment.

That is how long I've been creating. I colored in coloring books. I did all kinds of crafts in preschool. I even snuck underneath our big coffee table and colored the underside with all kinds of abstract colors and scribbles. (Luckily, I didn't get in too much trouble for it.)

My mom had a book for recording a child's school years, from kindergarten through high school. It had a place to paste school pictures and store report cards. It asked questions of the child at every grade, like, Who is your teacher? What is your favorite food? (Mine was always pizza, by the way.) Who is your best friend? What do you want to be when you grow up? Every year, I wrote down "Artist." (Well, other than in first grade, when I said "A teacher.")

As an adult, I realize that this conviction I had is more rare than common. When I was a child, I thought everyone knew what they wanted to be when they grew up and that some people pursue it and some don't get the chance. But I still thought the desire was there, deep in our hearts. Now I realize that many people don't have such a singular focus and never had a burning desire for one goal or passion early in life. I think that is why so many people are frightened and intimidated when they're asked, "What is your purpose?"

Talk about pressure! Most of us are just trying to live a decent life, pay our bills, and have a little fun on the weekend. Now we are supposed to find out why we were created and what our purpose is. (Cue freak-out here.)

Does Purpose Matter?

Is it that important to find our purpose? Does it matter to anyone?

I think it does. When I know my purpose, or when I'm on a mission to do something big, I jump out of bed in the morning, eager to start my day. I work steadily throughout the day, checking off each task and knowing that each one gets me closer to my goal or where I want to be. I feel alive and energized, and I am better able to navigate life's ups and downs when I know what I'm here on Earth to do.

I have seen the other side of not having purpose and the impact it can have on a person. I've seen people retire from somewhat meaningless jobs, thinking they're finally free to live a leisurely life. However, they often discover they lack a sense of purpose. With no compelling reason to get out of bed each morning, they can begin to feel lost. Their gradual decline often stems from not having a mission or purpose that sparks their mind and spirit, motivating them to embrace each new day. Without this sense of purpose, life can seem devoid of meaning, leading to a feeling of emptiness.

If existence is all there is, what is the point?

Maybe a life without purpose is prone to problems.

In working with entrepreneurs, I have found that almost every single one has a clearly defined purpose. Starting and growing a business is not the easiest path. If you are going to commit to this road, you'll have to have a greater purpose behind what you are doing in order to weather the storms that come with being a leader and business owner.

I believe that we are all wired for purpose. I believe each one of us has a divine calling for our life and a mission. Discovering that mission and purpose draws us closer to our creator and puts us on a path to a meaningful life. When we live with passion and purpose, the little stuff falls away. We gain a greater perspective on what matters. This allows us to consider our impact on this world and make a difference in the lives of others.

How to Find Your Purpose

There are wonderful books, classes, tools, and online tests to help you find your purpose. Most of them center on those feelings you had as a kid, when the whole world was in front of you and there were no judgments placed upon you yet.

If you are struggling with where to start, you can use these questions to spark a conversation with yourself:

- As a child, what did you want to be when you grew up?
- What was your favorite activity when you were a kid?
- What things came naturally to you when you were growing up?

- What topic can you talk about for hours and never get tired of?
- If you got to start over today and choose any career, what would it be?
- What activities do you love so much that you lose track of time?
- What would you do with your life if you had no fear?
- If you had all the money in the world, how would you spend your time?
- What do you love doing so much that you would even do it for free if you were independently wealthy?
- What would you do if you knew you could not fail?

Use a journal to work through these questions. Take your time. Invest in yourself and this process.

Personality Tests

A test that helps you learn how you are wired is another tool that can help you discover your purpose. There are dozens of personality tests, many of them free, that will help you discover who you are and why you act the way you do.

One of my favorites is the Myers-Briggs test: "The Myers-Briggs system consists of four preference pairs that reflect different aspects of personality—opposite ways to direct and receive energy through Extraversion (E) or Introversion (I), take in information with Sensing (S) or Intuition (N), come to conclusions using Thinking (T) or Feeling (F), and approach the outside world through Judging (J) or Perceiving (P).”[9] I am an INTJ through and through. When I first took the test and read my results, I couldn't stop laughing because it was *so* me! It is good to learn who you are and what makes you tick, then accept and embrace your uniqueness. From this healthy vantage point, you can discover all the special things that only you can do and the countless ways that only you can give back to this world.

Here are a few tests that many people find helpful:

- Myers-Briggs
- DISC
- Enneagram
- Wholehearted Inventory[10]

Try a few out, and see which one resonates with you.

I recently finished a book called *The Road Back to You: An Enneagram Journey to Self-Discovery* by Ian Morgan Cron and Suzanne Stabile. It is a wonderfully written book that uses the Enneagram as a self-discovery tool. The Enneagram is one of the most powerful tools for gaining insight to ourselves and others. It helps us understand our motivations, core beliefs, and unconscious patterns that drive our behavior. We have all nine Types in us, although one of the

---

9. "The 16 MBTI Personality Types," Myers & Briggs Foundation, myersbriggs. org, accessed May 23, 2024, https://www.myersbriggs.org/my-mbti-personality-type/the-16-mbti-personality-types/.

10. "Wholehearted Inventory," The Gifts Hub, brenebrown.com, accessed June 3, 2024, https://brenebrown.com/wholeheartedinventory/.

Enneagram Types is dominant for each of us.[11] For each of the nine Types, the authors begin the chapter with a description of what it's like to be that Type. They give twenty statements that describe that Enneagram Type so you can understand what this kind of person thinks and feels and how they behave and interact with the world. When I read mine to my husband, I couldn't stop laughing at myself. I am a Type One. Every single item on the list of twenty pertained to me. It was unbelievable.

The point of these tests is first to understand yourself. It helps to become aware and fully grasp who you are and why you do the things you do. The second point is to start to understand others and develop a greater sense of compassion for our differences, thereby allowing more grace into your interactions. There is no right or wrong personality Type. There just is. We are all made differently. We all have strengths and weaknesses. The goal when finding your purpose is to know who you are, what your strengths are, what ignites your soul, and how you can use all of that to make a difference in this world.

Ikigai

The Japanese have an amazing tool for helping a person find their purpose. The *Oxford English Dictionary* defines *ikigai* as "a motivating force; something or someone that gives a person a sense of purpose or a reason for living."

---

11. "Discover your Enneagram Type," The Enneagram Institute, enneagraminstitute.com, accessed May 23, 2024; "About The Enneagram Institute," The Enneagram Institute, enneagraminstitute.com, accessed May 23, 2024, https://www.enneagraminstitute.com/about/.

It can be most easily taught visually. So look at the diagram below.

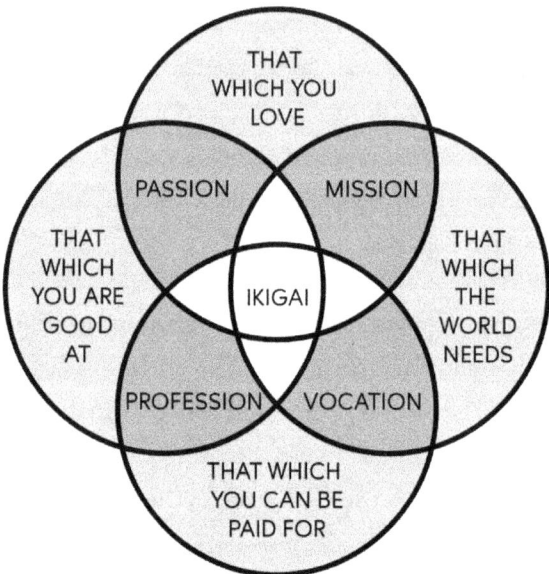

You can use your journal to write down your answers to these four questions:

1. **That which you love.** What do you love to do? What could you spend all day doing if you had all the money and time in the world? What brings you so much joy and happiness that time just flies when you are doing this wonderful thing?
2. **That which you are good at.** Write down all of your skills. Create a list of everything you are good at. If you are stuck, ask a friend or coworker what they say you are good at.
3. **That which the world needs.** Where do you see a need in the world around you? Where do you see a problem that

needs to be solved? Where are people hurting? Where is there injustice? Write down all the areas that you see the world needs right now.

4. **That which you can be paid for.** Now that you have these three lists, pull out some ideas of services, products, or solutions you can be paid for. Can you teach? Can you build something? Can you create something? Can you offer your skill as a service to someone who needs it? Get creative and keep writing down ideas.

Now, look back at the diagram and your lists of the things you love and the things you're good at. Which things are on both of these lists? Circle them. Those are your passions.

Then look at the things you love and the things the world needs. Which are on both of these two lists? Circle them. Those are your mission.

Now look at the things you are good at and can be paid for. Which are on both of these two lists? Circle them. Those show you your specific job or profession.

Next come the things the world needs and that you can be paid for. Which are on both of these two lists? Circle them. This is your vocation, which can be defined as the broader career field that you are called to.

Now, if you have filled in all four of the inner circles with one, two, or three words, is there one word that is in three or all four of the inner circles? If so, this is your ikigai. Now you know your life's purpose and have a tremendous gift in your hands!

My Purpose

In 2018, I spent an entire day with a life coach named Luke Kayyem. He gave us several different exercises to work on and worksheets to fill out. At the back of our packet was a blank page, and this is what I wrote:

> *I was put on this Earth to:*
>
> *Live a life of purpose and passion and help others do the same.*
>
> *To touch people's hearts and lives with my creative gift of art.*

These words came to me swiftly and easily, as if from outside myself. I still look at them from time to time. And although it didn't happen overnight, I know I am living my purpose today.

I want that same gift for you.

Purpose gives you clarity, focus, and direction. It imbues you with confidence and quiet assurance. It has a way of making the small stuff of life fade into the background and empowers your resilience.

Things That Distract from Purpose

People

There are so many things that distract from purpose. The biggest is other people's opinions. If you want to live your true purpose and calling, you'll need to let go of worrying about what other people think about you, your life, your vision, and your goals—all of it.

The only thing you can do is remain authentic, improve, and provide value every day.

You must also know that certain people won't understand you or your mission. Their comments will only drag you down. Sometimes, even the closest people in our lives can be real dream killers. When you are starting out on your journey of self-discovery and finding what your calling is, it may be wise not to share it with certain people in your life. You already know who they are: the pessimistic person, the sarcastic person, and the person who has never risked anything to achieve something great. Don't share your beginning with any of them. Choose only a trusted friend, business coach, or counselor when you need a little encouragement or support.

Perfectionism

I'm writing this one to myself. I will always struggle with perfectionism. It is tied somewhere to my value of excellence, but then I take it too far. I place expectations upon myself to be perfect, look perfect, do the perfect job for my clients, and be the perfect wife, daughter, or friend.

But guess what?

I'm not perfect. Not by a long shot. And I never will be, no matter how hard I try. Demanding this much of myself is counterproductive and not good for my insides. Age has a funny way of curbing this one for me. I have lots of gray hair. I have little spots on my skin, and my memory is not as sharp as it was at thirty. I am not what I used to be.

But that is okay. I am the best version of me here and now, and that is all I need to bring to the table each day.

If you are an Enneagram One like me, you'll fully relate to this. And if you are not, hooray for you! You will not have this particular burden to carry. You'll have a different version of it that you'll have to be aware of.

Some people need to know that getting something done is better than getting something perfect. Taking action is better than planning and thinking something to death. Let go of your personality's plan to self-sabotage your purpose-driven life. You do this by becoming aware of it and then saying no to it. Every day if you have to.

Control

"Some things are up to us, and some things are not up to us."
—Epictetus, Stoic philosopher

Ever since I was a little child, I needed to be in control. I think this was a reaction to my parents' divorce when I was six and life with my single mom, who struggled with depression. I had to grow up fast and take on more responsibilities than a little kid should have to. I have always been organized, on top of things, and very reliable at every job or business I've ever been involved in. People can depend on me to come through. Because of this, I tend to control things in my world. When people want to make plans, I set the date and time. I make a reservation if needed. When hosting a gathering, I cook and plan out the appetizers, desserts, and everything else so that the party flows well. I tend to take on too much and don't allow others to help as much as I should.

Here's what I have learned. Controlling everything will never work. And it will waste precious time on your way to living out your purpose. You have to allow things to unfold as they may in certain areas that are out of your control, and you have to allow other people to help you even if they don't do it the exact way you would.

Controlling everything is exhausting and will never bring about the beautiful, wonderful, joy-filled life you are longing to live. Accept people for who they are. Accept life for the chaos it brings. Stay in your own lane, focus on what you are meant to do, and let the other things either fall to the wayside or fall into place.

Next Steps

If you did not come out of any of these exercises with a clearly defined purpose, that is okay too. Purpose is, in many ways, a journey. And it is a wonderful and worthy adventure! Enjoy learning about yourself, who you are, what you love, and the ways you want to change the world. You will gain new insight and new direction by seeking this truth about yourself. Don't give up!

If you have a few ideas that you think might be your purpose but you can't decide which one it is, that is okay too. Start with whichever one fills you with the most excitement, and start pursuing this every day. Read books about it, talk to people who have already done the same thing, and write in a journal about your own experiences along the way. You may find it is a perfect fit, or you may decide it is not for you. If the latter is true, try another one of the runners-up and go all in with that mission. Action will lead to more discovery. That is the goal of pursuing a life of purpose.

If you are 100 percent convinced of your purpose and are ready to go, that is fantastic! I know you will change this world in wonderful ways and shine your beautiful energy on everyone you meet. Perhaps you will even be called to help others discover their purpose and passion along the way.

Books That Changed My Life

Called to Create: A Biblical Invitation to Create, Innovate, and Risk by Jordan Raynor

Big Magic: Creative Living Beyond Fear by Elizabeth Gilbert

Chapter 4 Action Steps and Resources

Ikigai diagram and worksheet

Chapter 5

Goal Setting

If you want to live a life of purpose, achieve great things, and know that what you are pursuing aligns with your values, then, in addition to having the right mindset, you'll need to set intentions or goals for yourself.

Goal setting is probably my favorite topic. I am an achiever, and that is most likely why I love talking about goals so much. But I think even in a mixed company, it is an energizing and positive topic to discuss.

When a friend tells me they are planning to start a business, my eyes light up, my posture changes, and all my focus is on them and how I can encourage them in their new venture. Goals are exciting. They move life forward. In a world where so many people want to wallow in complaints, lack, and negativity, I say, "Let's flip the script and talk about something of forward motion instead."

My favorite saying with goals is "If you don't write it down, it won't happen." I started writing my goals out many years ago, and I always taped them to the wall of my home office. When I was working at a company, I'd frame them and put them on my desk.

Look at your goals every day. Even when you are not consciously reading them, they are there in your peripheral vision, and something amazing happens. You will find yourself looking up and reading them intentionally one day and realizing how many you've completed. Or how many are just about to come to fruition without you having to strive, force, or make them happen.

On the other hand, there is power in intentionality. You need to take time to consciously move the needle, especially with your big goals. I think it is important to take time once a week, or at least once a month, to look at your big goals. Have a brainstorming session. Ask yourself, "What can I do today to take another step forward toward this goal? Can I call someone? Can I write to someone? Can I read a how-to book? Can I watch a how-to video? Can I fill out an application?"

Action moves things forward. Resist the urge to research something to death.

How to Set Goals

So, how do you set meaningful goals that move you forward to where you want to go?

Here is a goal-setting method I developed many years ago and have taught to others. It is very simple, and anyone can do it. Set aside some alone time to do this, and remove distractions. If you have an opportunity to be in nature, that is an ideal environment where your mind can dream.

Think. Dream. Plan.

If you haven't practiced goal setting before, the first step is to think, dream, and plan.

Take the time to look at your life. You can use a journal. Or, if you have access to a whiteboard, this is a great tool as well. When I'm doing this activity at home, I like to tape a giant piece of paper to the wall and use colorful markers to write down my answers and ideas.

Step 1: Think

Start out by asking yourself these questions:

- What do I want my life to be like?
- Who do I want to be as a person?
- Where do I want to live?
- How much money do I want to make?
- Where do I want to travel?
- Do I want to be married?
- What kind of business have I always wanted to build?
- What impact do I want to make on the world?

Allow your mind to dream and play without restrictions. Write it all down with joy and excitement in your heart.

After you have had fun dreaming and diving deep into all these different questions, it is time to refine things a little bit. Next, you will brainstorm about what you want to accomplish. Use these six categories to think about your entire life and what you'd like it to look like. You can create other categories if you like, but this is a simple way to capture the most important areas:

- Health
- Personal growth and learning
- Relationships and family
- Fun, recreation, and travel
- Business and financial
- Spiritual and giving back

Look at the first category and start writing, without any judgment, what you'd like to see, have, or experience in this area.

Here's an example of the first category:

- Have a strong, fit body
- Exercise five times a week
- Eat healthy foods
- Drink eight glasses of water a day
- Have a calm, centered mind

Here's an example of the business and financial category:

- Complete real estate broker licensing
- Close ten real estate transactions
- Hire a showing assistant
- Earn $185,000 in commissions
- Purchase two investment properties

Then, move on to the other categories until you have bullet points or sentences under each one. If there is another category you want, add that and repeat the same exercise.

Step 2: Dream

If you are having trouble getting started, close your eyes and imagine what your life looks like three years from now. Then write it out in story form.

- What is your health like?
- Do you meditate or do yoga?
- How do you look and feel?
- Are you learning a new language?
- Are you working on your inner self through therapy?
- Are you married? Are you single? Do you have kids?
- Who are your best friends?
- What do you do for fun?
- Do you travel to Europe or explore the US on road trips?
- What do you do for income?
- Are you a business owner?
- How much money do you make annually?
- How is your spiritual life?
- Do you volunteer?

Take the uninterrupted time to dream, imagine, and get into it. Don't filter anything. Just allow yourself to express anything you feel excited about in your future life, then write it out like a journal entry or a story.

Side note: These dreams might change over the years. You might look back at one you wrote ten years ago and laugh. I did! I wrote in 2008 that I wanted to live on two acres in Paradise Valley (a wealthy neighborhood in the Greater Phoenix area). I wanted an art studio, a music room, a gym, a pool, a pool house, and two offices for me and my husband. I wanted a pool service, a housekeeper, and a landscaper. And I wanted to drive a Range Rover.

WHAT?

I look back on that wish, and I don't want any of those things anymore. They are not aligned with my core values and the kind of life I want to live. But that is okay. We grow, we change, and we discover what matters to us and what we really want.

This year's dream board looks so much different. It is 2024, and I just want to be healthy and fit. I want to be an amazing wife. I want to travel with my husband. I want to inspire people. I want to help people build the business of their dreams. I want to create art. And, as I type this, I want to become a best-selling author.

Step 3: Plan

Once you have your six areas with bullet points or a written story about what you want for your life, read through what you've captured. From here, you'll create your list of goals.

Remember, focus on the *big* picture, not how to get there.

When you write your goals, always write them in the affirmative or positive, and write them as if they are already here.

Don't write, "I want to earn more money."

Write, "I am a successful business consultant, and I make $250,000 per year."

Don't write, "I want to lose weight."

Write, "I am healthy and fit, and I weigh 135 lbs."

There is power in speaking as if. Think of it as a declaration. Declarations have power, presence, and determination.

The dictionary defines the word *declaration* as "a firm, emphatic statement which shows that you have no doubts about what you are saying."[12] So, when I am writing out a goal, I'm not just going to kind of sort of talk about it. I'm going to stand up tall and declare it.

If you declare what you are going to do or have or be, you will power up that goal with everything inside you. You will shout it from the mountaintops and make it so.

Some examples of identifiable and achievable goals are:

- Buy one investment property and rent it out.
- Write the first draft of my book.
- Make $300,000 this year.

---

12. "declaration," *Collins Dictionary*, collinsdictionary.com, accessed May 23, 2024, https://www.collinsdictionary.com/us/dictionary/english/declaration#:~:text=A%20declaration%20is%20an%20official%20announcement%20or%20statement.

- Go on an amazing trip to Paris with my spouse.
- Successfully launch my online course.

Now that you've captured your list of goals, narrow it down to no more than five to ten goals to focus on in one year. If you have more, keep them in a Word document or a journal. Revisit them each year. I want you to achieve your goals and not get overwhelmed and give up.

Break It Down

The only way to achieve your goals is to break them down into bite-size pieces.

Look at your five to ten goals. What are they? Why do you want them? What will your life be like once you achieve them? Some of these are probably big. Maybe even BHAGs (Big Hairy Audacious Goals).

Now, we break each goal down into smaller pieces.

Let's say your goal is financial. You want to buy your first investment property. List all the things you'll need to do to step toward this goal.

- Meet with a lender to see what I qualify for and discuss loan programs.
- Explore the ideal area for rental houses in my price range.
- Determine how much I'll need for fix-up funds.

- Find an experienced real estate agent who works with investors.
- Save up for my down payment and closing costs.
- Interview property management companies.

This could seem overwhelming if you look at the list of six items. But let's pick one you can break down into smaller steps.

Goal Breakdown Example

Meet with a Lender

Step 1: Reach out to my network to find a lender who works with investors.

Step 2: Make an appointment to meet with them.

Step 3: Fill out a loan application and provide financials.

Step 4: Discuss what I qualify for and the different loan programs available.

Step 5: Get prequalified and begin looking online for properties in my price range.

Every goal can be approached this way. Our biggest dreams can seem so daunting at first. But when you break them down into steps, they are so much more achievable.

Goal Formula

Now that you've seen how to break down a goal, here is the formula you will follow to break down all of your goals into actionable steps.

- Deadline
- Larger steps
- Smaller steps
- Monthly tasks
- Weekly tasks
- Daily tasks using time blocking

Let's say I have an art show coming up in ninety days. Good news is, I have a firm deadline because I know the day and time when I have to show up at the gallery for opening night. Now I have to backtrack from there to see what I need to do to make this a successful show.

I will need to plan out both my actual paintings and my marketing. These are my large steps.

For my paintings, I know that I have committed to twenty new original pieces. These are my smaller steps.

I will need to create two paintings per week and leave the last two weeks for framing and finishing. To paint two paintings per week for the next ten weeks, I will need to time block my calendar with a minimum of four hours per day of painting, five days per week. This is nonnegotiable. Otherwise, I won't meet my deadline. That means I will need to say no to things that don't fit into my schedule.

I will need to map out my marketing plan for postcards, an email newsletter, and social media. I will also need time to name, photograph, and price my new artwork. I'll dedicate two hours per week to those tasks.

Here's How This Looks Using the Goal Formula

Deadline:

Date and time of art show opening: 5/15/25 at 7 p.m.

Larger steps:

Paintings and marketing

Smaller steps:

Outline the body of work for this show

Define the theme and overall style

Buy supplies

Create twenty new paintings

Coordinate with the framer to finish the artwork

Name each painting

Photograph each painting

Price list for all paintings

Title for the show

Design postcards

Update mailing list

Design email newsletter

Update the website with all new artwork and prices

Send out postcards

Create a social media content plan

Monthly tasks:

Eight paintings finished per month

Social media content calendar mapped out

Weekly tasks:

Two paintings completed per week

Two weeks for framing and finishing

Two hours of marketing tasks completed per week

Daily tasks, using time blocking

Four hours per day painting five days per week

Marketing activities scheduled on the calendar

When I am working on a big goal like this, I like to create some type of calendar on a wall in my studio or a whiteboard so I can look at my list every day and check things off as I complete them. It is a form of visual motivation. With this plan in place, I have no doubt that I will easily meet my goal and have a successful show.

Celebrate

It is so important to celebrate your wins.

I'm serious. If you reach your first milestone in a longer goal, take time out to celebrate it. Life is hard, and working on long-term goals is challenging. If you make a big deal out of accomplishing your wins along the way, you'll be more motivated to keep going.

When you've started a business, it is even more important. I started pursuing art as a business in 2011, and each December 10, I acknowledge my art business anniversary. Starting and running a business is hard work. There are so many days when you want to give up or wonder why in the world you ever took on such a daunting task. That is why we need to step back, reflect on what we've accomplished, and have a little party.

Visualize It!

Another fun way to reinforce your goal achievement is to create a vision board and hang it on your wall. This is a powerful tool that allows your mind to focus. Your subconscious will take in these images, and your reticular activating system will kick in! You can even do this with others in your family or have friends over and make a party out of it. Print images or cut up magazines. You can use images, words, numbers, or anything that creates a picture of what your ideal life looks like using the different categories you created at the beginning of the goal-setting exercise.

The Word *No*

Saying no is the part many people struggle with in relation to pursuing their goals. Successful people know that in order to accomplish their goals, they will have to say no to certain tasks, activities, and demands from friends, family, and coworkers. This relates to setting and keeping boundaries.

But it is also what keeps you on course. If you say yes to every exciting new opportunity along the path of your life, you'll never reach the finish line. You'll be too distracted to stay focused on what you set out to do in the first place. Being intentional about what you want requires you to say no to things that don't support that vision or goal. It may be slightly uncomfortable in the moment, but in the long run, you'll thank yourself.

Don't Give Up

I had to write this section for me as much as for you.

I am a driven person. I'm positive, and I don't quit easily. But even I can get beaten down with disappointment sometimes. There are days when I just want to give up. Those are the days when you have to find it somewhere way down deep inside to pause, realize what is really going on, and do something different to shake yourself out of this feeling.

When you are about to give up, it is usually when you are about to have a breakthrough. If you can draw upon all your strength to push through, keep going, and tap into your hope again, you'll reach your success on the other side so much faster and with much less frustration.

Annual Goal Planning

Every December, as I get closer to the new year, I start thinking about all the goals I'd like to accomplish. I generally get out my big notepad and colored pens, then I dream about the different areas of life. Personal growth, relationships, business, travel, finances, etc. I make my category headers in different colors, and I put on fun music.

Maybe I'd like to learn a language for a trip to Spain we are planning. Maybe I'd like to write a book. Maybe I'd like to expand my business. Maybe I'd like to start an accountability group for entrepreneurs.

This is a time for dreaming, fun, and joy. I make a few bullet points under each header, then I sit and ponder them. Are these what I want? Do they help me achieve my overall life goals? Would they make my year richer and fuller?

This way, I head into the new year with a list of goals that I am excited to accomplish. It sets the tone for my life and my business, and I use the same formula I showed you earlier to break each one down as needed. It's a great way to set yourself up for success.

Goals get things done. We have to know where we are going, then plot out the road map to get there. Setting clear and achievable goals provides us with direction and motivation. It acts as a guiding force through the challenges and uncertainties of life. By constantly reassessing and refining our strategies, we ensure that every step we take brings us closer to our ultimate vision of success.

Books That Changed My Life

You Are a Badass: How to Stop Doubting Your Greatness and Start Living an Awesome Life by Jen Sincero

Girl, Wash Your Face: Stop Believing the Lies About Who You Are So You Can Become Who You Were Meant to Be by Rachel Hollis

Chapter 5 Action Steps and Resources

Goal-setting worksheet

Goal-achievement formula

Quarterly check-in worksheet

Three-year vision worksheet

Chapter 6
Habits

Some people orchestrate their lives in a way that makes them happen. Other people wonder, *What happened?*

Do you ever wonder why some people seem to have it all together? They appear calm in a crisis. They are rarely hurried or rushed. Their lives look like they are in order and on track. After studying dozens of books and learning from many different entrepreneurs and leaders, I believe that the unifying element behind these successful people's lives is how they focus on their habits.

Why Do Habits Matter?

The human brain seeks out the path of least resistance. It is easier for it to function on autopilot. Good habits are the key to tapping into this function. If you create, practice, and maintain healthy habits, you'll improve your life and achieve your goals because you've given your brain an automated method to accomplish this. If the path to success is not automated and not part of a known routine, the brain will rebel against the newfangled thing you are trying to do and self-sabotage.

Habits are especially important when we are going through rough patches. If we are sick, stressed, or overloaded with work and worry, we can't possibly draw the strength to do new, healthy things even though we need them more than ever. If you establish good habits and routines when you are not pulled in twenty different directions, these systems will come through for you.

Even in the worst of times, habits and routines will keep you grounded. You will come out of your hard time even stronger. Hold on to this truth, and it will carry you through.

Morning Routines

I have always attributed my success and my ability to reach big goals to my daily routine. For me, it is essential. Especially in times of uncertainty, creating and establishing good habits in routines keeps me grounded.

A couple of years ago, I was coaching a group of young women in real estate, and I asked them if they had morning routines. They had not established this for themselves yet and didn't see the point. I countered with this fun fact. I said, "Do you know who has a morning routine? Billionaires! Billionaires have a morning routine."

It's true. Read biographies of successful entrepreneurs, and they will all tell you how much they guard their time and stick to their habits and routines. A busy business owner doesn't have the luxury of allowing their day to run away with them, leaving them scrambling to keep up. They need to control what they can and create a margin in the day for things they can't control.

You may not be a billionaire yet. But establishing a solid morning routine will help you achieve success in your day and your life.[13]

Here's how my mornings go seven days a week:

- Wake up at five thirty or six a.m. naturally.
- Drink water.
- Make coffee.
- Have quiet time with devotionals and prayer.
- Focus on gratitude.
- Review goals.
- Read something positive and growth-minded.
- Exercise.
- Meditate.
- Get ready for the day.
- Follow a meal plan.

My business tasks vary depending on the day. I write these out the evening before so I can just tackle them one by one and not have to try and plan when I should be working instead.

As you can see, my morning routine was crafted to set up my day for success. It helps me focus on positive and healthy things that will support me as I set out to achieve big goals in business and life.

---

13. Katya Kupelian, "9 billionaire morning routines, from Oprah to Mark Zuckerberg," Business Insider, November 9, 2020, https://www.businessinsider.com/billionaire-morning-routine-mornings-oprah-zuckerberg-bezos-musk-buffett-gates-2019-1.

Email

Nowhere in my morning routine was "Check my email." If you do one thing for your morning routine, allow yourself to wake up without technology. I used to make the mistake of running to my laptop or phone upon getting out of bed and being hit by the onslaught of problems before my eyes were even open. What an abrupt way to start the day.

We deserve to greet the day with a positive attitude, enjoy our coffee or tea, pray or meditate, or just come to life naturally without the negative effects of the outside world. Email can wait until you are at work or, if you work from home like I do, at least until you have determined that you are on the clock.

News

I like to be somewhat informed about the world, but not so much that it gives me anxiety and depression. If you are sensitive to crime, tragedy, and the toxic negativity the news media love to dish out, choose your news sources wisely, and choose how often you consume news during the week. Don't derail your morning by going so far down the rabbit hole of news that you forget all of your good intentions.

Make Your Bed

I know this sounds silly, but one of the best ways to start your day is making your bed. This simple act sets the tone for an orderly and neat morning. You show pride in your living space by keeping it neat. And it is a very easy first habit you can start!

If you struggle with keeping good habits, implement this one and keep it up for thirty days. Then, start implementing other simple habits. Over the course of a year, you will keep building on these basic foundations, and you'll discover that you have improved your home, your health, and, most importantly, your discipline—maybe without even realizing it!

I hope these ideas have helped you decide to establish your own morning routine that will help support your mindset, values, and purpose so that you can be in a prime position to reach your big goals. Remember, your daily routine will be uniquely yours. Try out a few different things until you land on a rhythm that feels good to you, helps foster productivity, and gets you closer to your goals.

How to Get Things Done

A routine is a set of habits all done together in a customary way. But how do you get things done when life throws unexpected things at you? Here's my simple method for staying on track during my busy days.

Let's Start at the End

Sunday evenings are review time:

- I look back on my week and see what I've accomplished.
- Then, I look ahead in my calendar and at my larger projects—sometimes several weeks ahead just to get the lay of the land.

- Next, I calendar out the week ahead and make sure all my days reflect the forward motion I am after.
- Then I write out my Monday tasks on my notepad.

I am a very tactile person, so although I love the computer for capturing calendar items and the Notes app on my Mac for capturing goals or things I want to review all the time, I still use an honest-to-goodness real notepad with paper and a pen to capture my daily tasks. I love writing them out the night before. I enjoy having my planner sitting on the right side of my desk so I can see it all day. And I love crossing things off. It makes me ridiculously happy.

I encourage all my clients to use whichever tool works best for them. If you love keeping everything digital, by all means, do that. If you love paper, buy an organizer and pen that you enjoy using each day.

The type of tool doesn't matter. The commitment to this daily habit does.

To-Do Lists

I keep my notepad on my desk so I can see what I need to accomplish. My goal is to have all items crossed off by the end of every day. This is realistic because I do not overload my day. I put tasks with reasonable timelines on the list. Why set yourself up for failure? That doesn't serve anyone. On occasion, an item does not get done, and that is okay. It gets moved to the next day.

Let's talk about that for a moment. You have to be self-aware and know if you can move a task once or twice and then get back on track or if you are moving your tasks over and over and never completing them. If you are constantly moving your tasks and never crossing them off, I have two questions for you.

Did you set yourself up for failure? Do you have unrealistic expectations for how long tasks actually take? If so, this is solvable. Time yourself doing a handful of your tasks this week. Write down the time you begin something and just work at your normal pace. When you are done, note the time you stopped. I used to have a tendency to think I could complete everything in half the actual time I needed. Once you pay attention to the time it takes to complete things, you'll set your day up with much less stress and have a sense of accomplishment at the end of each day.

Next, if you keep moving a particular task over and over each day, and then into next week, and maybe even to next month, you need to get real with yourself. Do you even want to do this thing? Does it even matter to you? Is it helping you reach your goals? Or is it just something you put on your list because you feel like you should do it? I have faced this one a few times. Now that I'm aware of it, I don't usually fall into this trap.

There was a book someone once told me to read. So I bought it, and it sat on my shelf forever. I kept staring at the book, hoping I'd get excited to read it, but I never did. One day, it was driving me crazy, so I picked it up and said, "I'm committing to reading this book."

Well, I got about halfway through, and I hated it. I stood up and threw it in my giveaway bag, and off it went to Goodwill. Sometimes, you just have to be honest about what you will and will not do. Life is too short, and sometimes you just need to get real and say, "I don't want to do this project or task or goal because it was probably never really my dream anyway!"

On the other hand, sometimes there are chores and tasks we aren't excited about, but it is, in fact, our responsibility to do them. That is not what I'm talking about here. When those are on your daily list, tackle them first. Suck it up, buttercup. You can't get out of these ones.

Supposedly, Mark Twain once said, "Eat a live frog first thing in the morning, and nothing worse will happen to you the rest of the day." No matter who said it, it is a gross expression, but it shows us how it helps to get the ugly things done first. Author and speaker Brian Tracy wrote a book called *Eat That Frog!: 21 Ways to Stop Procrastinating and Get More Done in Less Time*. In it, he emphasizes the importance of accomplishing the critical tasks in your day. For Tracy, eating a frog is a metaphor for tackling your most challenging task—but also the one that can have the greatest positive impact on your life.[14]

I see this most commonly with real estate agents when it comes to lead generation. Instead of tackling this task first in their day, they tend to delay it until it eventually falls off the calendar. Months later, they experience a lag in income because they were inconsistent in their lead-generating activities.

---

14. Brian Tracy, "Eat That Frog: Brian Tracy Explains the Truth about Frogs," Brian Tracy International, briantracy.com, accessed May 16, 2024, https://www.briantracy.com/blog/time-management/the-truth-about-frogs/.

If you procrastinate on the largest tasks of your day, you'll never complete them. You'll just keep moving them around your calendar until you feel frustrated and defeated. You don't want to live your life feeling like this. It is so much better to start your day by getting a great accomplishment out of the way first. It gives you confidence as you walk through the rest of your tasks, knowing you can do anything.

How to Form and Keep Good Habits

The biggest question most people have is not how to start a good habit but how to keep doing it consistently. Much like New Year's resolutions that fall apart before January ends, good habits can unravel quickly. Especially if you take on too many all at once. Remember that our brains are wired for protection and safety. When we try to start a new habit, the natural response is to resist it because change does not feel safe for our brains. It takes time to map out new neural pathways, so you can use these techniques to coax your brain into getting on board with your new habit.

In his brilliant book *Small Habits Revolution: 10 Steps to Transforming Your Life through the Power of Mini Habits*, Damon Zahariades lines this out perfectly. The author recommends instead of tackling a huge goal, break it down into smaller pieces and create a small habit out of that piece. Then do that habit every day for several weeks until it becomes routine. Then you are ready to add the next habit.

Here's a real-life example. During the pandemic lockdown, we enjoyed an at-home happy hour on more days than I'd like to admit.

Obviously, it was an unhealthy indulgence that I needed to tackle. Instead of telling myself I could never have a glass of wine again, I used the Small Habits Revolution method to turn this back into a more manageable pleasure and not an all-too-frequent occurrence.

I started with Monday. I told myself, "I never drink on Monday. Who would drink on a Monday? It's ridiculous to drink on Monday." With these new thoughts and a resolve to become healthier in this area, I easily incorporated this new healthy habit for several weeks. When this became routine, I decided to add Tuesday. "I never drink on Mondays or Tuesdays." Once that was ingrained in my mind and my life, I didn't even think about it. Then it was time to add Wednesday.

You see how the pattern works. Start so small that it is ridiculously easy to incorporate the new habit into your life, then add on from there. This way, your brain won't go into survival mode and resist all the good work you are trying to implement.

My Three-Step Plan to Create Automated Habits and Change Your Life

To make this even easier, I'll share with you the three-step plan I use to add a new habit into my life.

Step 1: Identify

The first step is to identify where you want to create a new automated habit. Using the questions below, ask yourself, What areas of my life am I dissatisfied with right now?

- Are you finding it difficult to manage your time effectively?
- Are you having a hard time converting leads in your business?
- Are you struggling to maintain a healthy lifestyle?
- Are you stressed from having to do everything in your business by yourself?
- Are you losing your temper with your family?
- Are you struggling to hit your revenue goals?

Now, take a moment to look over your answers. Ask yourself, If I could stop one bad habit, how would it make a positive difference in my life? Select just one of those things you would like to work on. Don't pick two. Don't pick three. Just choose one.

Step 2: Plan

Now that you have your one thing you are going to work on, you are going to flip it from a negative to a positive. Let's promote a behavioral change by creating a good habit.

Let's pretend you are struggling to maintain a healthy lifestyle. You've decided that if you could make some changes in this area, it would make a positive difference in how you show up as a business owner, a spouse, a parent, and a leader.

How can you flip the negative area of your life into a positive habit?

If you are overweight, choose losing weight, getting fit, or getting healthy.

Next, let's look at your options. Using our weight loss example, there are many different things you could do to lose weight. You could exercise. You could stop drinking alcohol, soda, or sugary drinks. You could eat healthy foods. This is where we have to get even more focused. It is too overwhelming to say, "I'm going to lose ten pounds in the next three weeks by exercising, not drinking, *and* eating salads."

While it is admirable to say you will start working out, eating a vegan diet, and eliminating alcohol, this is a recipe for failure. And, quite frankly, a meltdown. You probably won't make your goal, and you'll decide habits just don't work. So choose one habit you can start with, then track it every day until you don't even have to anymore because it becomes part of your life.

You can't succeed with an entirely new lifestyle all in one shot. Remember the old saying, "Rome wasn't built in a day." The same goes for making impactful changes in your life. That is why you take small steps to achieve great results. You ensure success by choosing something attainable. So, start with only one habit. Look at your list of possible options and choose just one. Which of these items can you commit to nonstop for twenty-one days with no cheating on yourself?

There has been massive research on how to make habits stick. One of the key factors is practicing the habit daily for a minimum of twenty-one days. I think thirty days can sometimes seem too long, and eight or twelve weeks definitely feels heavy. There is no magic formula to this number. It is just an achievable goal for you to start with.

Let's say you chose exercise. Now, you make a plan.

You decide that your new healthy habit is exercising more. You can say, "I commit to doing at least one twenty- to thirty-minute workout five days a week for twenty-one days."

Will you magically lose ten pounds by doing this?

Probably not, but you are not trying to reach the absolute end goal here. You are creating building blocks of progress and lifelong healthy habits that will get you to the end goal seamlessly.

Step 3: Act

The last step is, of course, the most important. You can plan and prepare all day long, but if you don't put your plan into action, nothing will get done.

Here are my top three strategies to take action effortlessly:[15]

1. Make it something you like.

The first part is to make sure you'll do it. It helps if you choose a method you like or are open to. If you love running more than anything, choose running. If you love yoga and Pilates, choose them. If you love being in a group fitness class where people hold you accountable, choose that. You know yourself best. Select the method that sets you up for success.

---

15. Adapted from James Clear, *Atomic Habits* (New York, NY: Avery, 2018).

2. Make it easy.

Creating a new habit takes effort. So, you want to remove any obstacles from your path. Here are ways to make your new exercise plan easy.

If you choose running, find a partner, and set up the days and times you'll meet to run.

If you choose yoga, sign up and pay for a package of classes so you know you are committed.

If you choose a group fitness class or a personal trainer, sign up and pay for that right away.

Then, enter the times and dates on your calendar, like an appointment.

Here's my real-life example: I have to work out by seven a.m. every day, or I won't do it. I know myself. If it gets past eight a.m., I am not going to do it. If you even think I'm going to work out after two p.m., you're crazy. Not happening. Ever.

You know yourself, so select the time of day you will be most energized to be consistent and accomplish your new habit. Put it on your calendar just like it is a doctor's appointment. You wouldn't just blow off your dentist or hair stylist or doctor appointment, would you? Don't blow off your appointment with yourself either. Your health, your happiness, and your goals matter deeply. Respect yourself by keeping your commitments to yourself.

3. Make it obvious.

Visual cues are another excellent tool. This is just a handy reminder to do the new habit you are working on forming. For example, when I was first incorporating exercise into my morning routine, I would lay out my workout clothes on my dresser the night before. That way, when I woke up in the morning, I'd see them and remember that after my coffee and prayer time, I was going to work out. This has become such a solid habit for me now that I don't even have to think about it. But it is still nice to have my workout clothes ready and waiting for me each morning.

I have my workout mat and weights sitting in my living room right by the TV. All I have to do is click a few buttons and roll out my mat, and I'm ready to go.

You can use this three-step plan to incorporate any new habit into your life. Just follow the steps and be consistent!

Celebrate

And the best part of all, at the end of your twenty-one days— celebrate! I'm serious. Take a moment to reflect back on your three weeks of doing hard work, trying a new thing, committing to a promise you made to yourself, and succeeding! Look at all the completed workouts on your calendar, the wear and tear on your gym shoes, and your fit and trim body. You did it!

You should be very proud of yourself and excited to stick with your new habit forever. Once it becomes so normal and natural that it is a part of your daily life, it is an automated habit. Creating a series of automated healthy habits is how you will reach your bigger goals and achieve the changes you have been seeking.

Habit Stacking

Once you have your first habit so solid and in place that you hardly think about it anymore, you can add a second habit. This works even better if the two habits are closely related.

S.J. Scott coined the term *habit stacking* in his book *Habit Stacking: 97 Small Life Changes That Take Five Minutes or Less.* He proposes that you "build routines around habits that don't require effort" because "small wins build momentum because they're easy to remember and complete."[16]

An example of this for me is exercising and eating right. Whenever I get done with a workout in the morning, I usually feel compelled to eat something healthy for breakfast. I'll admit that this one does not work every time. There are days when I override my judgment and have waffles, eggs, and bacon. But those days are pretty rare. The more healthy habits you incorporate into your life, the more healthy habits you will tend to stack on top of the strong foundation you've

---

16. Antoniette Gomez, "Habit Stacking - Making Wellbeing part of what you already do!" LinkedIn article, LinkedIn.com, April 15, 2020, https://www.linkedin.com/pulse/habit-stacking-making-wellbeing-part-what-you-already-gomez.

built. When you start seeing the benefits of the new life you've created, it will encourage you to keep going!

Habit Reset

Another fun tool is picking a day of the week when you want to reset and refocus on all the good habits that keep you on track and happy. I developed Self-Care Saturdays, and my husband invented Me Mondays. On Monday, he weighs himself in the morning, drinks lots of water, eats healthy foods, and works on his mindset. Sometimes, he will go for a bike ride or a gratitude walk in the park—anything that focuses on good and healthy habits that he wants to make a priority.

On Self-Care Saturday, I like to go for a walk or bike ride, listen to an entrepreneurial podcast, or read an art magazine or business book. These all make me feel good and connect to what is important to me. You might enjoy this fun routine of choosing a day of the week when you get to focus on what matters to you.

Don't Beat Yourself Up

I am writing this section for myself as much as for you because I can be so mean to myself.

When you miss a workout, eat a candy bar instead of a salad for lunch, or drink too much and go to bed with makeup on, please don't beat yourself up.

We are all human, and none of us is perfect. You are going to make mistakes. You are going to have moments of weakness. You are going to have days when it is just too hard to stick to all of your well-intentioned good and healthy habits.

It is okay. Just get back up and try again. Don't use a one-time or one-day backslide as an excuse to go off the rails and eat cake for breakfast and quit the gym. Just start again. Start again at the next meal. Start again the next morning. Start again with the next healthy habit in your day. Beating yourself up and wallowing in guilt and regret will only make it worse. Just acknowledge it, recommit, and move forward.

Take Time to Rest

For those of us who are go-getters, always on the move, and reaching for the next goal with a thousand things on our to-do lists, here's a little reminder.

Take time to rest.

I have a tendency to stay constantly busy. Before a walk, I might throw in a load of laundry to be extra efficient. If we are going out to dinner, I'll be answering emails until the last minute. I often try to squeeze extra productivity into our downtime.

In my mind, there's nothing wrong with this. I'm just being my productive self, getting a hundred things done in a day. However, after twenty years of marriage, I'm beginning to see my husband's perspective.

When do we rest? When do we take a walk without multitasking? When do we sit and talk without my phone's constant interruptions? When do we simply get to be?

Strive for progress, not perfection. New habits take time to establish and become ingrained.

Take a day off and just read, walk, go for a drive, or enjoy a magazine or favorite book. Allow your body to unwind and your mind to be at ease.

Reflect on your progress, and be thankful for how far you have come.

Books That Changed My Life

Atomic Habits: An Easy & Proven Way to Build Good Habits & Break Bad Ones by James Clear

Chapter 6 Action Steps and Resources

Habits worksheet

Habit tracker ideas

Chapter 7
Health

Feeling good and maintaining a healthy lifestyle is vital as you forge ahead in building your business and pursuing ambitious goals. Optimal health is the foundation upon which you can achieve your dreams and fulfill your purpose. With a positive mindset, aligned values, and a clear sense of purpose, you can set meaningful goals and develop productive habits. This holistic approach ensures that you not only pursue success but do it in a way that is sustainable. After all, without good health, it becomes much more challenging to reach your potential and live out your purpose.

When I speak about this kind of health, I mean the kind that you can control. What foods are you putting into your body? Are you moving your body every day? Are you reducing stress by getting enough sleep and making time for rest?

These are all things that are up to us to take care of each day to ensure we are living a healthy life.

"Take care of your body. It's the only place you have to live."—Jim Rohn

Exercise

Let me start this section by telling you that I am *not* an athlete. I can't stand playing games, I can't run or play a sport, and I never have.

One of my earliest memories of not being athletically inclined was field day in elementary school. All the other kids loved field day and waited expectantly for it each school year. But this was the day I dreaded. Instead of having classroom time on field day, we all went out to the sports fields to get some exercise. There were relay races, long jumps, high jumps, and sprints. Each kid had to participate in seven to ten athletic activities. They pinned this round laminated circle to our chests, and at each event, we would get a colored ribbon stapled onto our badge to show where we placed in the event.

Well, being the nonathletic kid I was, all of my ribbons were lime green. That's lime green for last place. Yep, field day was the stuff of nightmares for this introverted, artistic, studious child.

I was nearly thirty when I had to face the reality of working out because of my chronic back issues. My chiropractor insisted that exercise was the only way to alleviate my pain. Using his favorite fitness book, he printed out exercises, highlighted the ones for me to do, and outlined the reps and weekly frequency. He advised me to start with low weights, track my progress, and increase as I got stronger.

His kindness changed my life.

I faithfully hit the gym three times a week, following his plan. Slowly but surely, I felt stronger, and had much less pain.

Exercise became a part of my life forever.

During the pandemic, with gyms closed, I discovered a free workout app called FitOn. I now use it every morning and enjoy a wide variety of workouts, from yoga to Pilates, strength training, and cardio. In nice weather, I take a walk or ride a bike every morning, and if life gets busy and I have to miss a day of working out, I'll still take a twenty-minute walk just to move my body.

Fitness has become one of the most important things to me because I know the value it adds to my life. You don't have to have any athletic skill whatsoever to move your body every single day if you are physically able to do so. Walk, ride a bike, hike, do yoga, join a class, join a group, go to a gym, or do whatever makes you happy while you are working on your health. I can tell you firsthand how much this matters.

Food

I grew up with a single mom who didn't enjoy cooking. It was also the late 1970s and early 1980s, so fish sticks and TV dinners were all the rage. In general, we maintained a relatively healthy diet. There was rarely ever a fast-food night, and we never had soda or candy in the house. When I first started dating my husband, we cooked together but used a lot of processed foods as side dishes, not knowing any better. In our early years of being married, he enjoyed cooking, and I liked to clean. It was a great trade-off. I didn't have confidence in my own cooking skills at that time. Along came Pinterest, and I started looking up recipes and saving them. We would watch cooking shows, and I started learning how to chop vegetables and sauté things, along with all kinds of other new techniques I had never learned. Soon, I started trying out new recipes, and they turned out well.

We have also learned a ton about nutrition and what fuels our bodies and have incorporated fresh fruits, vegetables, whole grains, lean meats, and healthy snacks into our daily lives, significantly improving our health.

Food can be challenging. It can trigger emotional responses, be a comfort or even an addiction. I love food, and I think there is nothing better than gathering with friends over a fantastic meal. I don't do well on diets, cleanses, fasts, or any of that. We each have to find what is right for us.

Wherever you are on your food journey, I hope you find balance and peace with it. Prioritize health over a certain size or number on the scale, and your compass will always point in the right direction.

Water

Every time I read about a health and wellness coach emphasizing the importance of drinking water, I laugh a little bit only because I was born and raised in Arizona, and I can't drive one mile down the street without having a water bottle in my car. I have a Yeti cup full of ice water with me at my desk, in my studio, in the car, at an appointment—yes, everywhere I go. We just can't function without drinking water in Arizona.

But for those of you who don't live here and don't have this desperate need for hydration like we do, drink your water. It is incredibly good for your body and helps your skin too! I have never been a soft drink person, and I don't drink fruit juices or tea. So after my morning coffee, I drink only water all day long. On certain nights, I enjoy a couple glasses of wine. Pretty basic, but it works for me.

Sleep

I don't struggle with this area, but many people do. Getting a quality night's sleep is so essential because it enables the body to restore. It is linked with stress reduction and even weight loss. If you have trouble with this area, here are a few tips.

- Create a sleep routine. An hour before bed, start preparing your mind and body for rest. Wash your face, brush your teeth, put on your pj's. Put your phone away on the charger. Close your laptop. Put on relaxing music, and get comfortable on the couch. If you like to read, pick up a good book. Maybe even darken the room and light a candle. Do whatever rituals help you feel calm and relaxed. There are even nighttime meditations you can try too.
- Make yourself go to bed at the same time. This helps your body get used to this routine.

- Don't have any electronics in the bedroom. Have just a cozy, warm, and comfortable bed waiting for you to drift asleep on. Waking up feeling good after a wonderful night's rest is an amazing feeling.

Progress, Not Perfection

Bill Phillips is quoted as saying, "Focus on progress, not perfection."[17]

I can't love this quote enough. As an admitted recovering perfectionist who's still trying to kick this nasty personality trait, I must remind myself of this every day.

It is even more important when we're discussing health. You're a human, not a robot. You are going to slip up and have dessert at a party, an extra glass of wine with a friend, or a deep-dish pizza when traveling in Chicago—duh! And you need to know that it's okay. You are going to skip a workout day when you don't feel well. You are going to get off track on occasion. The key is to focus on your progress and get back on track the very next day, the very next meal, or the very next workout. Just because you had a tiny setback doesn't mean you should quit trying.

We need to encourage ourselves and each other to keep going, keep trying, and know that some days, eating that chocolate chip cookie was the best we could do. But tomorrow, we'll eat the salad.

---

17. Bill Phillips according to "Focus on progress not perfection," AZ Quotes, azquotes.com, accessed May 23, 2024, https://www.azquotes.com/quote/858321#google_vignette.

Comparison

In your health journey, it is important not to compare yourself to other people. Honestly, looking at photos of someone twenty-five years younger than you who only eats egg whites and tuna and works out three hours a day will not make you feel good about yourself. Love the body you are in, and commit to the level of health you know you are capable of. Let the comparison game go. That will only hinder you.

I have fit friends I'll see on social media running a half marathon or winning weightlifting competitions. I applaud them and encourage them for their accomplishments. My joints do not respond well to running, and my body does not love extreme heavy lifting. I have to choose different exercises that my body likes.

We are all differently abled, and that is okay. Embrace where you are and compare yourself only to where you were yesterday. That is how true progress is made.

Stress

What Stress Can You Eliminate?
We all know that life comes with stress. When you're an entrepreneur, life comes with lots of it. The medical community reminds us how toxic stress is for our mental and physical health, so it is important to address this issue.

Take some time to do a life audit. Start with your calendar. Are you adding more stress to your daily life by taking on too much?

Everyone in America loves to wear their busyness like a badge of honor, but it can be detrimental to your well-being. Start with your schedule and get real with yourself. Are there any items you can eliminate, maybe not forever, but for the season of life you are in so that you can reduce your stress and focus on your health?

Next, do a social media audit. Scroll through your Facebook or Instagram feed or whatever else you are using. As you look at images, text, or a certain person or group, does any of it give you a bad feeling? If so, unfriend or unfollow right now. You do not need a daily dose of toxicity. This negative influx is damaging your health. You may not think it is, but it is there in the back of your mind or in your subtle emotional response. Remove from your social media anything that doesn't make you feel good and uplifted.

Or, even better, if you can live without a certain social media platform, delete your account. My husband deleted his Facebook account a few years ago, and it changed his mornings. By removing the injection of negativity first thing in the morning and filling that space with positivity instead, he now begins his day without the burden of anger or irritation. This simple adjustment has significantly improved the overall tone of his daily routine.

Next, audit your television consumption. Are you watching happy and positive shows, or are you drowning in drama, the news, violence, and other negative viewing patterns? Much like how the food we consume either helps or harms our bodies, the media we consume helps or harms our heads. Be very aware of what you allow into your mind.

Reframing Stress

We will never be able to eliminate every form of stress. That just isn't a realistic expectation. So, we have to train ourselves how to deal with its presence.

It has taken me decades to reframe how I respond to stress. There are still days when I have a complete meltdown because too many things stack up against me. The important lesson is how to respond to stress rather than react to it.

Let's say a driver cuts you off on the freeway. The natural response is to scream and yell and honk the horn and maybe throw out some swear words. This is a reaction—a knee-jerk emotional outburst following a perceived attack. Over time, reacting in this way adds to our stress and isn't healthy for us.

Next time, after the initial shock and fear, just breathe deeply, turn up the radio, and continue driving. Don't give it a second thought. Be grateful that you are safe, and go on with your day. Gratitude is the most powerful response we can have, even though it may sound crazy. But there is scientific proof of the health benefits of gratitude.

An article from BYU says,

> "Research has shown that feelings of gratitude correlate with increased energy, improved mood, and health benefits. In one study, those who completed a gratitude journal spent nearly 1.5 hours more per week exercising, reported feeling

more joyful, enthusiastic, interested, energetic, excited, and strong, and they helped others more. Those who were taught appreciation exercises experienced more coherent heart rhythms that enhance communication between the heart and brain, had an increase of levels of immunoglobulin A (a defense against sickness), had a reduction in levels of cortisol (a stress hormone) and an increase in DHEA (a hormone that reflects relaxation)."[18]

On days when I am struggling with multiple issues that all seem to pile up on me and am feeling my stress levels rising, I try to stop and take a moment to reflect on what is real. Oftentimes, I write down the four or five things I'm upset about. Seeing them so small on a sticky note diminishes their power over me. After that, I get a grip on perspective. I take a moment to be grateful for my health, my home, my husband, and my many blessings, and I just breathe.

Sometimes, I compare my difficulties with those of people I know who are struggling with cancer, mental health issues, relationship problems, or anything that is so much larger than what I wrote down on my tiny piece of paper. Other times, I reflect on those in other parts of the world who are experiencing great persecution, extreme poverty, or famine. None of my troubles can compare to that level of stress. Getting a true perspective usually recenters me and helps me be grateful for the small problems I actually have.

---

18. "Gratitude Journal and Attitude," BYU Comprehensive Clinic, comprehensiveclinic.byu.edu, August 19, 2019, https://comprehensiveclinic. byu.edu/gratitude-journal-and-attitude.

People

Whether friends, family, coworkers, spouses, neighbors, or strangers, people can bring added stress to our lives. As much as we love and need connection, relationships are hard. This may seem odd to write about in a chapter on health, but how you interact with people affects your health. If your closest relationships are full of turmoil, your mental and emotional health will be too. Eventually, what is going on inside will start to affect the outside, including your physical health. I am no expert in this area by any means, but I'll be happy to share what has worked for me.

Boundaries: Setting and enforcing proper boundaries is a helpful tool for reducing stress in relationships. You need to be very confident and comfortable in knowing who you are, what is valuable to you, and what you are willing to do and not do. You also need to be strong enough to say this to other people. Those of us with people-pleasing tendencies struggle with setting boundaries more than others do, but it is a skill we all must develop in order to have a healthy and happy life.

As an entrepreneur, one example of a boundary you might need to establish is being able to say, "I will not respond to work-related calls or emails after eight p.m. in order to prioritize personal time with family."

This boundary ensures that you maintain a healthy work-life balance by setting clear limits on when you are available for work-related communication. It allows you to recharge and dedicate quality time to your personal life outside work hours.

111

Communication: Healthy communication with family and friends plays a crucial role in reducing stress and fostering emotional well-being in your busy life. By openly expressing thoughts, feelings, and needs, you can strengthen relationships, gain support, and create a sense of connection that provides comfort and resilience during challenging times. Regular communication allows you to share burdens, celebrate achievements, and maintain a healthy balance between work and personal life, ultimately contributing to greater overall happiness and fulfillment.

Slowing down: Slowing down and savoring the present moment can reduce your stress. Here are some things I love to do when life is too chaotic and I need to reconnect:

- Read a book
- Read a magazine
- Go for a walk in nature
- Lie in bed with the windows open
- Watch the sunset
- Listen to music
- Go for a bike ride
- Make a cappuccino or cup of tea
- Go for a scenic drive
- Sit on the patio and just rest

Make your own list, and keep it handy when you are feeling stressed and need to take some time to settle your soul and recenter yourself.

As you continue your journey toward a healthier lifestyle, may you prioritize self-compassion and find what works best for you.

Remember, your well-being is worth investing in, and every step you take gets you closer to achieving your overall goals, pressing into your values and purpose, and cultivating habits that support your long-term dreams.

Books That Changed My Life

Boundaries: When to Say Yes, When to Say No to Take Control of Your Life by Dr. Henry Cloud and Dr. John Townsend

The Five Love Languages: The Secret to Love That Lasts by Dr. Gary Chapman

Chapter 7 Action Steps and Resources

Health plan

Stress-reduction ideas

Chapter 8

Finances

Money is the number-one topic that couples fight about. Money issues can ruin friendships, business partnerships, and relationships, and yet young people are taught so little about it in school. I was never taught about money. I think we tend to pick up our views and beliefs about money in childhood, and many times, these vague concepts stay with us throughout our lives, whether they are correct or not.

The views on money I acquired from my two parents were vastly different.

My father was born in Berlin after World War II. It is a miracle he survived as an infant and toddler. He lived in a city torn apart by war and had very few resources to survive. He eventually had three other siblings and recalls his mother making cabbage soup on Sunday with different vegetables and no meat. This one pot of soup would have to last the family of six an entire week. So, by the end of the week, they were surviving off of broth.

Because of growing up this way, my father decided he was going to be rich. He moved to America in his early twenties and became a citizen and an entrepreneur. He owned several different businesses and did quite well for many years. He bought real estate and owned several Mercedes-Benz cars, an RV, and even a couple of boats. His poverty experience pushed him to dream big, take risks, and never doubt his ability to have a better life than his family did.

My mother grew up the youngest child of three and spent her early years in New York and the rest in Arizona. Her parents were of the Greatest Generation and lived through the Depression. My grandfather served in World War II, and my grandmother stayed home with the kids because she was stricken with polio in 1950. They were responsible and frugal people. My grandmother sewed dresses for my mom and cooked delicious food. They lived very simply and did not splurge on material things. Going out to dinner after church was their one luxury for many years.

My mother's outlook on life is very different from my father's. She sees the world through the lens of lack. There is never enough money to last, and you have to be careful with what you have.

My parents split up when I was six, and I was raised by my mom. We lived very simply. Over the years, we lived in two single-wide mobile homes, a few different houses, and an apartment. When I was in elementary school, my clothes often came from a thrift store or were hand-me-downs. We didn't have much, but we always had food on the table and a roof over our heads. The bills were always paid by my hard-working single mother. We spent vacations in Show Low,

Arizona, where we stayed with my grandparents or my aunt and uncle. Once or twice, we got to go to California. Our special treat was going to dinner once in a while at Taco Bell. I still remember my order: a bean burrito, a crunchy taco, and a small orange soda for $2.13. Mom always got the tostada. It wasn't a hard life. I had a loving mom and a good family. It was just a life lived with the knowledge that we didn't have money, so we couldn't have certain things.

I developed an interesting view of money as a young adult. I viewed my father as reckless and risky. He always had at least one hundred-dollar bill in his wallet, and usually lots more. He ran businesses and was the boss. He lived in a "mansion house," in my opinion, and had lots of cars and nice things. He could go on vacation wherever he wanted to, but since he was a workaholic, he rarely did. I didn't see him as having an abundance mindset (because I had no clue what that was).

At the time, I subscribed more to my mom's view of money: a lack mentality. I got jobs that paid minimum wage. I was careful not to spend money on anything that wasn't a need.

I distinctly remember when my parents told me they couldn't afford to pay for college. I was in middle school at the time, and they explained that I better get good grades and earn a scholarship if I wanted to go. I was a straight-A student and graduated high school with a 4.17 GPA (weighted due to advanced placement classes), so I earned several grants and a partial scholarship to art school.

I went to art school in Denver and lived with three wonderful girls in an apartment. As an only child, that was a new and challenging experience for me. I worked a full-time job and went to school. There was no money left over for anything.

Twelve months into my college experience, things shifted. My financial aid counselor called me into her office to let me know the government had taken away my Pell Grant because I made too much money.

I stared at her, completely stunned. I was going to school full-time, working full-time, paying for a room in an apartment, and paying my basic bills to live. I certainly wasn't making "too much" money. I could barely eat.

She explained that my only choice was to apply for loans. But I was opposed to the idea of burying myself in debt at age eighteen. I just couldn't do it. So I made the agonizing decision to drop out of art school and move back home to Arizona. It crushed me to give up on my dream of getting a Bachelor of Fine Arts degree, but I couldn't make sense of leaving school with $50,000 in debt and an art degree.

My mom was gracious and allowed me to move in with her for a little while. I got another minimum-wage job and took every art class I could afford at community college.

Whenever I was too low on cash and needed to buy something, I'd get creative. I'd dig through my room and search for things to sell. I was always able to part with something I didn't absolutely love or need in order to get cash for the item I had to buy. I started a side business painting children's murals for people. I was so young and inexperienced that I worked way too hard and charged way too little. It wasn't sustainable for me. It wasn't until I got sick and tired of working nights and weekends in retail that things started, very slowly, to change.

First, I got a job leasing apartments. It was a bit of a pay raise, and the hours were much better. After a few years of that, I moved into my first admin job at a property management company. I loved the Monday-to-Friday, nine-to-five schedule. No holidays and weekends at work anymore! I started to learn new computer and business skills. It was 2000, and the Internet was changing things in the world of business.

I ended up quitting my admin job and went to work helping my dad with a start-up he was working on—this new thing called eBay. He was selling home projectors and projection screens, and he needed help. I started by handling all the packing and shipping. Then I started learning about eBay and how it worked. I enrolled in college classes on web design and earned an AA in computer science in twelve months. I was like a sponge and couldn't wait to learn the next thing I could use to help grow our business. I read *Entrepreneur* magazine, attended seminars and trade shows, and learned everything I could about small business. By 2002, Dad and I had grown our business to a million-dollar company.

I'd love to tell you that everything kept growing and we got richer and richer every year, but that is not what happened.

Dad and I kept running the business, but the revenue decreased a bit each year after that peak. In 2003, I married my amazing husband, Paul, and I wanted to make a change in the business. Dad agreed, and I split off and ran my own version of the business by myself so I could work from home and make my own executive decisions on how I wanted to run the business and my overall life now that I was married. I made a modest income and had time freedom. I loved it.

Until 2007, when I got a phone call from a customer who was looking for a specific projection screen. I pulled the info up and quoted him a price.

He replied, "But I can buy it on CircuitCity.com for fifty-seven dollars with free shipping."

This price was significantly lower than my price. In fact, it was even better than my dealer's price. I quickly pulled up the competitor's website and saw the shocking truth right there in front of my eyes. All I could say to the customer was, "Yes sir, yes you can. Have a nice day."

I hung up the phone with a pit in my stomach and knew that my small business was over. I called the manufacturer I purchased my screens from and found out that they had opened the floodgates to Sam's Club, Costco, Circuit City, Best Buy, and all the other big box stores—something they had not done in fifty years of being in business. They didn't warn us small mom-and-pop businesses. I'm sure they didn't care. But I watched a business I'd built for seven years die in one afternoon. It was a hard pill to swallow.

For a few weeks afterward, I lay on the couch, watched mindless shows, ate chips, and kind of went numb for a while. I had no idea what to do. I didn't want to go back to admin work. I didn't want to go back to retail. What was I going to do with my life? How was I going to earn money?

My husband had a brilliant idea. At the time, he was an appraiser, and we were just starting to become interested in real estate investing. We were using other real estate agents to help us look for and buy our first property. He said to me, "You love school. Why don't you get your real estate license?"

Thus began the real estate chapter of my life.

I went to real estate school and loved it. I got a 97 percent on my school exam and then passed the state and national tests. I was so proud! I was an official REALTOR! But here is the truth no one ever tells you: just because you graduated and have a license doesn't mean you have a clue as to how to actually sell real estate, much less run it as a full-time business.

I hung my license with a big brokerage that provided lots of free classes and marketing help. They were wonderful. But I still didn't have a single client.

Being a born student, I started learning everything I could about being a successful entrepreneur. I checked out tons of books from the library and researched real estate investing on the Internet.

My husband and I drove to San Diego for a Maui Millionaires seminar. I remember it cost $1,500 for our tickets, and I had to scrape together everything I had so we could go. We stayed in the cheapest motel we could find and soaked everything in like sponges. This was such a crucial step in changing our mindsets from being employees and agents to being entrepreneurs. Every seminar I went to led to another book, another entrepreneur, and another workshop. I did anything I needed to expand and grow as quickly as I could.

At this time, we also joined a local real estate group to learn more about getting started in investing. We were on several email lists from different investors. Paul encouraged me to answer an ad looking for a licensed real estate salesperson for one of these investment companies. I decided I had nothing to lose and applied.

I got the interview on October 31, 2007. I went into it without any attachment to the outcome. If they offered me the job, great. If not, I'd keep exploring my options. They ended up offering me the job, and I helped grow that company from the ground up, starting with a handful of independent contractors to over fifty employees and agents generating millions of dollars in annual revenue.

It was quite a leap from where I'd started. I didn't even know how to enter a real estate listing or answer another real estate agent's questions when I began. By the end, I was handling some of the most complex transactions in the industry and participating in panel discussions to train others on how to do what we did. It is amazing how life has such unexpected turns. I made more money at that company than I'd ever had. I like to joke that I got my PhD in real estate.

I worked with some pretty amazing people while we built this incredible business together. We fueled each other's growth by sharing books we were reading, attending seminars and workshops, and exchanging ideas. All of that led to changing my money mindset.

In 2011, the market shifted, and I told the CEO I was going to quit and go paint. I wanted to get back to my first passion, which was creating art. At the same time, I conducted multiple real estate transactions during the worst market in Arizona, but more importantly, Paul and I also bought more rental properties. We didn't have traditional corporate jobs. No 401(k)s for us. Residential real estate became our retirement vehicle of choice.

In 2014, I fell into another start-up real estate investment company and helped the two founders build it from the ground up. My superpower is taking entrepreneurs' crazy ideas and turning them into something we can implement and bring to fruition. It was a wild ride that lasted all the way through 2020. But when COVID-19 practically stopped investors from buying real estate, I parted ways with my dear friend and business owner, and for the first time, I took an entire year off.

In 2021, I created art, read books, went for walks, and took an amazing two-month road trip across the US with my husband. It was the first time I wasn't on call to write contracts or coordinate a real estate deal. It was amazing to feel so free!

Although I loved having an entire year off, I knew in my heart that I was meant for more.

In 2022, I did some consulting work for another real estate investment start-up while spending time discovering what I wanted to pursue next. Having the freedom to ask that question—to explore what I was destined to do with all my skill sets, knowledge, and experience—opened up a whole new door for me.

That statement I wrote down in 2018 kept on whispering to me, and I knew I had to act on it this time.

I was put on this Earth to:

- Live a life of purpose and passion and help others do the same
- Touch people's hearts and lives with my creative gift of art

I had wanted to do coaching and consulting work for other entrepreneurs for years. I love helping others bring their business ideas to life, and I finally had the time and space to invest in this dream. By 2023, I was able to launch my coaching business. Now I am writing this book to help even more people discover their purpose.

Nuts and Bolts

It was important for me to share what I've gone through in relation to money so you understand the journey I've taken to write from this perspective. I think a lot of times, authors and entrepreneurs make it look effortless because they've come so far and learned so much. But we were not there for that part of their story. We only get to see the successful and shiny result of decades of hard work. Now that you know where I came from, I'll teach you some of the nuts and bolts I have used— and still use—to maintain a successful money mindset.

Simple Budgeting

I never learned to budget. Neither of my parents taught me how. My high school didn't offer a class in life skills (although I think every high school should). Here's how I learned how to budget. You can do it too.

Step 1: Download your bank statements from the last three months. If you use cash, use your Notes app to record exactly what you spent your cash on each day. Do this step for a minimum of thirty days.

Step 2: Get a notebook or Excel spreadsheet, then record every single penny you spent and organize your expenses into categories. Examples: groceries, gas, rent or mortgage, clothes, shoes, beauty (shampoo, makeup), eating out, dry cleaning, etc.

Step 3: Add up the total of each category. Then, add up all expenses and average them for thirty days.

Step 4: At the top of a notebook page or Excel spreadsheet, write your take-home pay and any other income you get each month. Total the income. Below that, total the expenses and their categories.

Step 5: Subtract your expenses from the income. If you are in the positive, congratulations! Now you can add other categories, like savings. That is the fun part!

If you are in the negative, this is where the real work begins.

Now you have your first budget. Let's review and make sure you have some tools to ensure success.

In Steps 1 through 3, you recorded and categorized all your expenses. The key here is to be realistic. If you are spending $150 per month on clothes or $500 per month on eating out, write that down. Don't write down a smaller number and tell yourself, "I'll do better." You won't. You will only set yourself up for failure.

In Step 5, you were faced with the reality that you are doing an amazing job at spending less than you earn or that you need to make some adjustments. If you are like most of us, it is the latter. And that is okay. In fact, it is very normal in our American culture. This is where you have to get real with yourself. You have to take a hard look at these categories and your spending, then find out where you can cut back and where you can't. Use the sample budget I created for you in the book resources.

First, take a look at fixed costs. These are things like rent or mortgage, insurance, car payments, utilities, and any bills that are pretty much the same every month and that you can't live without. Set those off to the side. These are not areas where you can negotiate with yourself unless you intend to sell your car or downsize your home.

You're going to spend some time on your variable costs. Clothes, shoes, eating out (including coffee), entertainment, travel, Amazon shopping, home decor, hair, beauty, gifts, and even groceries all fall into this category. These are areas where you can reduce, cut back, or even eliminate expenses to balance your budget. Only you can decide what your nonnegotiable items are. What can you live with? What can you live without or have only as a treat?

Here are a few of mine.

I love a pedicure in a salon. It is so lovely to have someone soak and massage my feet and paint my toenails perfectly. But it can be expensive. So, most of the year, I do these at home in my bathroom. Thankfully, I'm an artist, so painting my toenails isn't that hard. Every once in a while, I'll treat myself to a pedicure. It is a nice treat but not a monthly expense I'm willing to add to my budget.

I sometimes pull back on eating out. Don't get me wrong, I love going out to eat. I rarely got to do that as a child, so it is a big deal for me as an adult. However, if I am saving up for something or paying off debt, this is an easy category to cut back on. First of all, it saves money. Second, it saves my waistline from all those calories. Third, my husband and I cook amazing food, so eating at home is often way better than eating out.

Where are some areas you can cut out or cut back? Once you've assessed your categories and created a balanced budget you can live with, be prepared to update it for the first few months once real life kicks in. You may have forgotten a category that happens once a year. Or maybe you're surprised by a jump in gas prices. It's okay. Just update it and adjust.

Basic Business Budget

You can use this exact same method for your business. Follow the steps listed above and apply them to your sales, service, or commission income. Track all your business expenses. Then, check to see if your business is profitable.

As a business owner, tracking your profit margin is an important way to test the health of your business. Profit margins vary greatly in different business sectors, so do some research to see what an average number is for your industry. Then you'll know if you are low or high. Adjusting your pricing, number of sales, or number of clients can help you increase your bottom line. Knowing your numbers is crucial for an entrepreneur and will help you as you set your business goals each year.

If your personal or business finances are not where you'd like them to be, you will have to find ways to maintain the integrity of your monthly budget.

Saying No

If you are new to budgeting, you also may be new to saying no to friends or even family. You will have to strengthen this muscle because you can't say yes to everything and stay within your budget.

That doesn't mean you won't have fun. You just have to look at things a bit differently. Instead of going out to the bar with your friends and spending sixty or eighty dollars or more, invite your friends over to your house. Wine and beer are a fraction of the cost when purchased at a local store versus at the bar. If you want to have a fun dinner with friends, skip the pricey restaurant and do it at someone's house.

Ignore Ads

This is probably pretty obvious advice, but you must train yourself to ignore advertising.

> "Back in 2007, market research firm Yankelovich ran a survey of **4,110** people and found out that **an average person sees up to 5,000 adverts every day.**
>
> Today, that number is even higher, and the **average person sees around 10,000 ads per day**, though only a quarter of that or less will be relevant."[19]

Stop being a product of consumerism! You are literally buying into the lie that you must be in debt to be happy. You get to choose where you spend your dollars, not where the fashion industry tells you, not where electronics companies tell you, and not where huge marketing companies tell you.

This one is even more real for entrepreneurs. We are bombarded with ads and pitches for online courses, monthly memberships, and exclusive coaching programs that promise to increase your income

---

19. Nadia, "How Many Ads Do We See a Day?" Siteefy, siteefy.com, updated April 25, 2024, https://siteefy.com/how-many-ads-do-we-see-a-day/#:~:text=Back%20 in%202007%2C%20market%20research,or%20less%20will%20be%20relevant.

to $50,000 months, $100,000 months, or eight figures a year. I'm sure many of these are extremely valuable for the right person at the right time in building or scaling business. But use discernment in finding the right fit for your business—especially if you are just starting out.

Money Mastery

Many of my coaching clients struggle with their business finances and end up using their business bank account like an ATM card. This is a common scenario with my real estate clients primarily because their income fluctuates so much. Often, they do not pay their estimated quarterly tax payments and end up with a nasty surprise from the IRS the next year. You'd be surprised at how many high-income-earning entrepreneurs do not have a bookkeeping system or even a CPA.

Here are a few tips for taking control of the financial component of your business:

Step 1: Keep your business checking account and personal accounts separate. Never commingle these funds. I recommend having a separate business savings account and business credit card as well.

Step 2: Hire a bookkeeper or develop a weekly bookkeeping system for your business, and be consistent with it. Knowing your numbers is key.

Step 3: Hire a CPA who specializes in your industry. I only hire CPAs who are very familiar with real estate investments because they know the best tax strategy for my exact needs.

Step 4: Set aside a percentage of your income for taxes (ask your CPA about this), and set aside a different percentage into a savings account to prepare for shifts in the economy. Talk to your tax professional to create a plan for your life and business.

These are just a few basic ways to start if you haven't yet developed a financial strategy for yourself.

Marketing for Free

There are countless low-cost ways to get the word out about your offering. Using social media, writing blog posts, networking, and teaching classes are just a few ways to market your business when you don't have a large marketing budget yet.

Life Lessons in Building Wealth

If you are interested in moving beyond the basics of budgeting and want to build long-term wealth, here are a few key lessons to incorporate into your life.

Have an emergency fund: There are amazing books out there that will teach you valuable core principles, but one of my favorites is *The Total Money Makeover: A Proven Plan for Financial Fitness* by Dave Ramsey, the creator of *The Dave Ramsey Show*. He teaches the seven baby steps of money management.

Step 1 is to create an emergency fund of at least $1,000. It is shocking how many American families do not have $1,000 set aside for unexpected life events like accidents, health issues, and auto repairs. This is a critical first step in managing your money and your life.

His other six steps are equally as important, so definitely pick up his book or take his course to learn this entire program. It is solid advice, especially for those carrying debt.

Pay yourself first: If you commit to this one principle early on, you will be astonished at how far it will take you. Pay yourself 10 percent of your take-home pay, and put it in an account for investing. At first, you'll simply develop the habit of sacrificing this amount and setting it aside in an account. Over time, your goal will be to seek wise counsel on how to invest. You'll need to learn how to take calculated risks, not reckless gambles. Learn the life lessons needed to make your money work for you. My husband and I chose to invest in real estate. But there are other areas to invest in. Go with the wise advice you receive from trusted professionals who have built wealth, then choose the method that works for you and your family.

Own your own home: This life lesson is becoming lost in America. Currently, the national rate of Americans who own homes is around only 65 percent. That means a large percentage of people do not have control over a huge monthly expense because their rent can go up at any time or they can be forced to move because of a change in the landlord's situation. They are also not building equity, nor do they have as many tax deductions as a homeowner does. I know it is not easy to save up a down payment, maintain good credit, and have a stable job that ensures you can pay the mortgage every month. But if you are able to make this important move, it is worth it.

Plan for retirement. This goes without saying. You might be young, fit, and agile today. But one day, you won't be. And you won't be able to earn income. You need to plan for retirement while you are young. If you don't, it will sneak up on you, and you will not be prepared. The most tragic thing is to have too much life at the end of your money.

My husband and I chose real estate as our retirement vehicle. It offers both immediate cash flow and the potential for long-term appreciation. Real estate may not be the retirement vehicle of choice for you. Discuss it with your family and your professional advisors, but put a plan in place that ensures a stable future.

Contentment

I do not think you can discuss finances without bringing up contentment. Our materialistic American society hates this word, as does every marketing company out there that's trying to entice, seduce, or scare you into purchasing their products. However, I feel it is my responsibility to bring the concept to life in this chapter.

Let's talk about what contentment is not. It is not settling for less than. It is not giving up all worldly belongings and living in poverty. It is not going through life grumpy and dissatisfied. It's the opposite, really.

Contentment is being grateful for all your blessings. Contentment is wanting what you already have. This does not mean you can't have goals, desires, and ambition. It means you embrace where you are at and what you have, and you develop an attitude of gratitude for how abundant your life really is.

Then you look at your budget and discuss with your partner or family if a big purchase is necessary, responsible, and a good and sound decision. You don't get sucked into the trap of consumerism, which tells you that you are not enough unless you buy more, more, more. Our culture tells us we are not beautiful enough if we don't buy designer apparel, makeup, skincare, and hair products. You are not healthy enough if you don't buy the pharmaceutical drugs in every other commercial, and you are not successful enough if you don't drive the latest, hottest car. Read through what these shiny and polished ads are selling you, and don't fall for it.

You are strong enough to make financial decisions for yourself and your family that have nothing to do with keeping up with the Joneses or your ego. Look around and be grateful for where you are. Set goals and a savings plan for when you want to purchase something at a bit of a stretch, but don't do it for anyone else. Live by your values, and you will have great freedom.

Generosity

Depending on how your childhood formed your relationship with money, generosity may have a good connotation or a negative one. My husband has a very generous mother. She is always thinking of others, cooking or baking something delightful to share, and being a thoughtful gift giver. My husband is the same. He always makes time for someone, helps someone, and hosts gatherings at our home to cook and enjoy time with friends.

I grew up in a household where I developed a mindset of scarcity. We were cautious about giving too much because our resources were limited. While this was true monetarily, the underlying sentiment is not something I want to live with anymore.

It has taken many years of mindset work in the area of finances. I thought that money was hard to come by and I better keep it if I got it. When I began unraveling my past limiting beliefs about money and learning how to rewire that part of my thinking, it changed my entire perspective on money and giving. I desire to give generously to organizations that align with my values, and I am able to do this through my business funds as well.

When you realize you can't keep any of it anyway, it changes your perspective.

My husband and I recently completed our estate planning. We don't have children, so legally, we have no heirs. We have worked way too long and hard to have our money end up where we don't want it to go, so we invested time and money into an estate plan. Now we get to choose what will happen when we die and what organizations and people we want to bless with our funds.

My husband looked at me joyfully one day and said, "I feel so much better because we've given it all away." Even though the giving technically doesn't happen until we pass away, on paper, it is all gone. And we feel so good about who it will go on to help after we depart.

Another interesting thing happened during this estate planning time. I was sitting in the living room and looked around the room at the paintings on the walls, the furniture, the books, the dishes, our photo albums, and our wedding photos. I realized, with a bit of shock, that we have no heirs and, therefore, no one to give any of our belongings to. Not just meaningless things like chairs and tables, but the story of our lives in photos and memories and the things that matter to us now.

Let me tell you, when you realize that all your stuff is going to end up in a dumpster one day, it changes your perspective on how you view things. What am I going to invest in? More dishes? More decor? More stuff? Probably not. I am, however, going to enjoy my home and the things I do have here and now, and focus on creating meaningful experiences and memories.

Money Mindset

It took me *years* of work to change my money mindset. I'll be honest. I still struggle with it from time to time.

I doubt my abilities, I lose my confidence, and I shrink back into lack mode. Once I witness myself doing this, I have to shake things up and get a grip on what is really happening. But with each setback, I've learned to recognize the patterns and pull myself back into an abundance mindset. It's a journey, but it's worth every moment of self-discovery and growth.

Books That Changed My Life

Rich Dad Poor Dad: What the Rich Teach Their Kids about Money That the Poor and Middle Class Do Not! by Robert Kiyosaki

Smart Couples Finish Rich by David Bach

The 4-Hour Work Week by Timothy Ferriss

You Are a Badass at Making Money by Jen Sincero

Chapter 8 Action Steps and Resources

Simple budgeting worksheet

Chapter 9

Time Management

I live by my calendar, not in a controlling or negative way but in a way that brings me both joy and success. I plan my workout times and morning routines. I plan appointments and meetings. I plan business tasks and projects. I also plan fun events like date nights, vacations, and friend time. I have learned over the years not to over-plan it. Otherwise, it becomes overwhelming and leaves no room for spontaneity. But I do use my calendar daily, and I enjoy it.

If you don't control your schedule, someone else will.

What does that mean? If you have a blank calendar and are living your life as carefree as can be, others might see it as an opportunity to insert their agenda into your day.

"Hey, I need a ride to the mechanic. Can you take me?"

"Hey, I left my wallet at home. Can you pay?"

"Hey, I heard you are going on vacation. Can I crash at your house while you're gone?"

I'm not talking about the times when you're genuinely happy to help a friend out. I'm talking about the importance of having a plan for our life and your day so others don't fill your time with their agenda.

People who are on a mission, growing a business, and pursuing a purpose do not have time to constantly rescue others from their mishaps. They prioritize their goals and ensure their schedule reflects their mission and accomplishments. It is okay to say no. It's okay to have priorities and stay committed to your path.

Living with purpose and intention, and ensuring your calendar aligns with your goals, is key to success.

Being Realistic about Time

This may sound odd, but I don't think people know how much time things take. I often see my clients make the mistake of cramming too much into their daily calendar and either doing a poor job on each task, stressing, hurrying, and rushing through their day, or not getting everything on the calendar done.

I have a simple tool that will help you learn the reality of time.

Clock yourself doing everything for one day or week until you get a sense of the truth about your tasks. How long does it take to get ready for work in the morning? How long does it take to cook dinner, enjoy eating it, and do all the dishes afterward? How long does it take to perform a key task in your business?

How long does it take to write five hundred words for your next book?

Just track all the everyday tasks that are on your calendar and jot down the time it took to do them for a week. Afterward, review the results. You'll be shocked at how many things take so much longer than you thought.

Once you have this data, print out a blank daily calendar page or use a notebook, and write out an ideal day and the times in the left-hand column. Write down your ideal average day. Like a Monday.

What time do you wake up? How long do you enjoy coffee and quiet time? Do you work out in the morning? When and for how long? Map out your entire day, and see what you are dealing with. From there, you can make adjustments so your days are set up for success.

Here are a few ways to gain control of your schedule and become a master of your time.

Eliminate

Are there any areas of your life where you are wasting time doing things that don't matter? Are you scrolling social media for an hour? Are you watching too much TV? Are you doing things in your business that make you feel busy while, in reality, you are not accomplishing anything that moves the needle? Identify the time wasters and eliminate them.

Delegate

Are there any tasks that you are not amazing at doing? Can you delegate them? Chores the kids can take on? Bookkeeping you could hire a professional to do? Marketing tasks you could hire a company to take over? If you are not 100 percent the best and most skilled person for the job, can you find someone else to take it off your plate so you can focus on fulfilling your highest and best purpose?

Purposeful Time

Once you have eliminated the time wasters and delegated the routine tasks, take a hard look at where you can carve out much-needed time blocks. Can you wake up an hour early? Can you give up a social event that you don't even enjoy? Where can you find time to do what matters in your long-term vision of your life?

Time Blocking

Time blocking can be difficult for some people. I do well with a to-do list. I don't necessarily block out a specific time slot for a specific task, but some people love managing their time this way.

I have trained many clients in the sales industry. Because the nature of their business is reactive, time blocking can be especially difficult for them. The best approach is to block out larger chunks of time for basic sales tasks and day-to-day life, knowing you may have to adjust and reprioritize on a daily and weekly basis. The key is to not let the tasks you reprioritize completely fall off the schedule. Instead, move them to a day when they will get done.

168 Hours

We all have 168 hours every week to sleep, eat, work, and play.

When you say, "I don't have time for that!" it's not true.

It's not because you don't have *time*. It's because it's not a *priority* for you.

Your task is to use your favorite calendar tool—(Google calendar, iCal, or a day planner)—to block out the seven days in your week, hour by hour.

7 AM Workout & Get Ready	7 AM Workout & Get Ready	7 AM Workout & Get Ready	7 AM Workout & Get Ready	7 AM Workout & Get Ready
8:30 AM Lead Generation	8:30 AM Lead Generation	8:30 AM Lead Generation	8:30 AM Lead Generation	8:30 AM Lead Generation
		12 PM Client Lunch		
1 PM Listing Appointment	1 PM Marketing		1 PM Social Media Plan	

Start by blocking in your top-priority tasks. If you work in sales, enter your lead generation time blocks. If you are a full-time mom and have school drop-off or kids' activities, put those in first.

Combo Similar Tasks

Find a few days each week to time block and combine similar tasks:

Try to group all client meetings into one or two time blocks per week to make your schedule less scattered.

Rather than running small errands individually throughout the week, designate one day to complete them all. This saves time and energy by reducing the number of trips you have to make. It also helps you stay organized by tackling similar tasks in one go.

Instead of dealing with finances sporadically, set aside specific days each month to review and manage your finances comprehensively. This could include tasks like budgeting, paying bills, reviewing investments, and updating financial records. By consolidating these tasks, you can gain a clearer understanding of your financial situation and make more informed decisions.

If you regularly produce content, such as blog posts, social media updates, or videos, schedule dedicated time blocks to brainstorm ideas, write drafts, edit, and finalize content all at once. This approach can help you maintain consistency in your content output and streamline your creative process.

Pad Your Time Blocks

We all think tasks take a shorter amount of time than they actually do. In order to keep on track throughout the day, pad your time blocks. If you think it will only take thirty minutes, schedule an hour. Trust me—this will help immensely! Padding your time blocks and appointments will allow the day to unfold naturally. Even with those little emergencies that sneak into the day, you will still be able to accomplish 90 percent or more of what you had planned on your list.

Don't Overcommit!

One of my best tips is to stop squeezing a million things into each day or week. Overcommitting your time will only stress you out and ensure that you do *not* accomplish the things that matter to your long-term goals.

Why Am I Really Doing This?

I ask myself this question about things on my calendar or things I'm about to commit to. It makes me stop and rethink before saying yes. Is this going to further my goals? Ask yourself, "Can I delegate this? Or is it something I can eliminate?"

Guard your time! Say no to things you don't need to be doing.

Review and Reprioritize

Because of the reactive nature of our busy lives, you will have to shift things around to make room for the high-priority items. Make it a daily habit to review and reprioritize nonurgent items and move them to a better day. Every Sunday evening, make it a habit to plan out your week ahead using your time-blocking skills.

Procrastination

We can't discuss time management without dealing with the elephant in the room—that sneaky beast called procrastination. It's known as "the act of delaying or postponing something." This is ironic because most of us know procrastination as the opposite of action. There are many theories, tips, and tricks for ending procrastination's deathlike grip, but I think we must first understand the root of the problem.

Procrastination often shows up because of fear. Let's say you set a goal to double your business's revenue in the next year. You're pumped and ready to crush this goal. You buy the latest software, hire a marketing expert, and invest in business coaching. But when it's time to put those plans into action, you hesitate. You delay making that crucial sales call. You postpone launching that new campaign. You procrastinate.

Why do we do this to ourselves?

Because we are scared. We're scared we won't hit that revenue goal. We're scared of potential failures along the way. We're anxious about losing money on new investments. We're worried about the challenges that come with scaling the business. This fear can paralyze us, whether we're dealing with business goals, personal development, or financial aspirations. It's the fear of the unknown and the fear of the steps it will take to become the successful person we want to be.

But I have good news. There is a way out of this self-sabotaging loop. You can stop procrastinating by taking action. Jump up and do it anyway. Do it right now. Do it before you even have time to think. Use Mel Robbins's brilliant 5-4-3-2-1 method, and launch yourself like a rocket out of bed and into immediate action, then go do it.[20] Keep doing this every morning until it becomes a habit. Once it

---

20. Mel Robbins, *The 5 Second Rule: Transform your Life, Work, and Confidence with Everyday Courage* (Houston, Texas: Savio Republic, 2017).

becomes an automated, unconscious habit, the fear is gone—and the procrastination is too.

You can do this! I believe in you.

Other Helpful Tips for Time Management

Morning or Evening

Whenever I'm coaching people on time management, I start by asking them this very simple question: "Are you a morning person or an evening person?"

We all know the answer right away. I happen to be a morning person. I jump out of bed ready to greet the day. I have my coffee and devotional time, go for a walk or bike ride, work out, meditate, get ready, and have breakfast. Then I work diligently on my tasks for the day.

I love doing everything I possibly can before noon. I probably get more done in a day than most people do in a week. But that's me, and I love it. Being productive and efficient with my time makes me happy.

However, if it is after four p.m., don't ask me to do much. By then, I am ready to wind down, read a book, or relax by listening to some music on my patio. I might have a nice conversation with my husband or head to happy hour with some friends. I will prepare and cook dinner, do the dishes, and clean the kitchen, but I will not accomplish anything amazing after four. Productivity after dark? No way.

So, what kind of person are you? Are you the kind that sleeps in? Or do you feel all your energy after two p.m.? Are you able to stay up until one a.m. creating amazing work? Many people are wired this way, and that is fantastic.

It doesn't matter which type you are. You just need to embrace it and then time block your day around it. If you are writing a book and are an evening person, then perhaps your best writing time is ten p.m., when the kids are asleep and the house is quiet. If you are an evening person, you may want to go to the gym at six p.m. and crush your workout.

Don't fight who you are. Just work with it to maximize your day. It will feel much more intuitive to work within your body's time clock than to push against it and try to meet someone else's schedule.

Be Selective with Your To-Do Lists

I want to put twenty-five things on my daily to-do list. I totally do. I want the joy and pride of crossing them all off at the end of the day and saying, "Wow, I did it!"

But that is no reason to drive your family or friends crazy. Be selective.

When you are creating your to-do list the night before, ask yourself, "What are three things I can do tomorrow that will move my business forward? If I got those three things done, I would be so proud of my accomplishments, and the rest of the day would fall into place."

Write those three down. Now, of course, you will have other things, like personal errands, but let's knock the three valuable ones out of the park.

If you do this every day, you'll have completed twenty-one important items by the end of your week. If you do it for a month, you'll have finished ninety amazing steps toward your goals.

And if you want extra credit for rest, you can focus on the three things only five days per week, and you'll still be crushing sixty tasks that matter for your business or your life goals every single month. That's amazing work right there! That is something to be proud of while still allowing time and space for self-care and your loved ones.

This concept comes from the Ivy Lee Method.[21] It dates back to 1918, when Lee, a productivity consultant, was hired by Charles M. Schwab, the president of the Bethlehem Steel Corporation, to improve his company's efficiency. As the story goes, Lee offered his method to Schwab for free, and after three months, Schwab was so pleased with the results that he wrote Lee a check for $25,000—the equivalent of about $400,000 today.

The Ivy Lee Method

This is a simple method for achieving peak productivity:

1. At the end of each workday, write down the six most important things you need to accomplish tomorrow. Do not write down more than six.
2. Prioritize those six items in order of their true importance.

---

21. Mark Abadi, "A CEO and dad uses a 100-year-old strategy to get control of his schedule in just 15 minutes each night," Business Insider, businessinsider.com, September 8, 2018, https://www.businessinsider.com/ivy-lee-method-productivity-2018-9. https://jamesclear.com/ivy-lee.

3. When you begin your day in the morning, concentrate only on the first task. Work until the first task is finished before moving on to the second one.
4. Approach the rest of your list in the same fashion. At the end of the day, move any unfinished items to a new list of six tasks for the following day.
5. Repeat this process every workday.

You'll notice that I reduced my method to only three important items because I think six is a bit overwhelming for most of my busy entrepreneurial clients. You can choose whatever number of items works best for you and your life.

Use a Timer

During the pandemic, I found it difficult to make myself go into my studio and paint. This seems counterintuitive to me since I had all the time in the world. But perhaps all the mental and emotional uncertainty was causing me some uncharacteristic procrastination. So I decided to make myself go into the studio for one hour per day. I started by pulling up a stool and sitting there staring at my half-finished painting. After a few minutes, I would get up, walk across the room, and start painting. Before long, an hour had gone by, and I found myself happy and productive.

Try the one-hour method and see if it helps you dedicate time to a focused project or task you've been putting off. It may help. Or you may be more excited to try The Pomodoro Technique.[22]

22. Laura Scroggs, "The Pomodoro Technique," Todoist, todoist.com, accessed May 16, 2024, https://todoist.com/productivity-methods/pomodoro-technique.

The Pomodoro Technique was developed in the late 1980s by then-university student Francesco Cirillo. Cirillo was struggling to focus on his studies and complete assignments. Feeling overwhelmed, he asked himself to commit to just ten minutes of focused study time. Encouraged by the challenge, he found a kitchen timer shaped like a tomato (*pomodoro* in Italian), and the Pomodoro technique was born. Here is a summary of the steps:

1. Get a to-do list and a timer.
2. Set your timer for twenty-five minutes, and focus on a single task until the timer rings.
3. When your session ends, mark off one Pomodoro and record what you completed.
4. Then enjoy a five-minute break.
5. After four pomodoros, take a longer, more restorative fifteen- to thirty-minute break.

This is a great method, especially if you are working on something you don't love. I use it when I have to prepare my taxes each year. I usually dread this chore, so I break it up into thirty-minute chunks. Then I put it away for the day and start again on a different day or week that I have logged in my calendar. By the time a week or two have passed, my tax packet is prepared and ready to send over to my CPA.

Music

I sometimes get myself moving on a task or chore by putting on one album. An album of music is often about an hour. I choose a favorite, click Play, and start painting in my art studio, writing, or working on a big project. Before I even know what happened, the last song ends, and I'm shocked that all the time went by so quickly.

Touch Things Once

Although I've focused this section on time and how to manage it better, I can't help but mention David Allen's amazing book *Getting Things Done: The Art of Stress-Free Productivity*. If you struggle with time management, you must read it. One of its key concepts is the rule of touching things once.

Imagine you're working on a project and receive an important email. Most people glance at it, decide to deal with it later, and then it gets buried under a pile of other tasks. This delays progress and adds stress. Instead, follow the touch-it-once rule.

Here's how it works. You open the email and immediately decide its fate. Is it a quick reply? Do it now. Is it a document you need to review? Save it directly into a specific folder dedicated to documents that require your attention. If it's an invitation or appointment, add it to your calendar right away. And if it's irrelevant, delete it immediately.

This simple rule will save you so much time. Touch each item only once. Address it immediately and then get back to what you were doing. This minimizes clutter and keeps your workflow smooth and efficient.

The faster you can make decisions with anything that comes across your desk or into your inbox, the better you'll be at time management and the more productive you will become.

Eliminating Distractions

I think one of the reasons so many people struggle with time management is that there are so many distractions and interruptions in their day. Whether it is family, friends, coworkers, the phone, emails, text messages, or social media notifications, we are experiencing a constant barrage of interruptions, which makes it extremely difficult to get anything done. If you work in an office, there may not be a whole lot you can control to guard your workspace from distractions, but here are a couple of suggestions.

Communicate your needs: Be honest with your boss and coworkers about needing a quiet space so you can finish your project or task. Ask them not to disrupt you during your time blocks. Ask that they request a scheduled meeting instead.

Shut down your email: Ignore or turn off your email while you are working in your focused time. That way, you won't get pulled into other tasks, questions, and conversations.

Silence your phone: Put your phone on Do Not Disturb or silent mode and put it in a drawer. You will still receive text messages and voicemails, but you won't be tempted to answer them. If you are using time blocks of thirty minutes or an hour, you won't be out of reach for very long in case something urgent does come up.

If you are one of the many employees or business owners working from home these days, you will have to contend with a different set of distractions. It could be a spouse, kids, pets, deliveries, or a neighbor. Not to mention laundry, chores, and other household things that call to you. The first rule, again, is communication. Let your spouse know when you are at work and ask them to not interrupt you during this time. If you have a door to your home office, close it so you can be at work. Chores and laundry will have to wait until you are off. Don't be tempted to turn on the TV and fold clothes instead of finishing the report that is due by five p.m. Communication is also key when dealing with family, friends, and neighbors who think that because you are at home, it is social time.

When I need to focus during my time blocks, I shut down my email and silence my phone. I'll even put it in another room so I can't reach for it. I don't look at social media during work time unless I'm using it for a marketing task—and again, that should be time blocked.

In our culture of super-connectivity, it is imperative to guard your time and use it wisely. Otherwise, you will find yourself at the end of an eight-hour day saying, "What did I even do all day?" You want to end your day on a good note, feeling productive and proud of your accomplishments.

Becoming a master of time management is another critical skill in living a life of purpose and achieving your big, beautiful goals. It is just another habit you can cultivate over time. The more you practice it and choose the tools that work for you, the easier it will be to maintain this momentum.

Books That Changed My Life

Getting Things Done: The Art of Stress-Free Productivity by David Allen

Chapter 9 Action Steps and Resources

Delegate-and-eliminate worksheet

Priority matrix worksheet

Chapter 10

Self-Discipline

This has probably been the number-one key to my success—sitting down and doing what needs to be done when I don't feel like it.

Mel Robbins said, "Fact: You're never going to feel like it. Ever. But you have to #DoItAnyways."[23]

When I read that quote, I burst out laughing. But I appreciated the blunt truth of her statement. Do I *feel* like eating a salad instead of a pizza? *No.* Do I *feel* like doing a thirty-minute workout instead of lying on the couch reading a magazine? *No.* Do I *feel* like doing social media for my business at certain times? No, but I sit down and get to work and do it anyway.

Self-discipline is what separates your success from your excuses.

Here's the harsh reality of life: Most people won't take action to do what it takes to make their dreams come true. Most people aren't

23. Mel Robbins (@melrobbins), "Fact: You're never going to feel like it. Ever. But you have to #DoItAnyways." Twitter post, Twitter.com, February 25, 2019, https://twitter.com/melrobbins/status/1100089048683765761?lang=en.

willing to sacrifice, work those extra hours, or do things that are not their favorite in order to have what is best for them.

The easiest way to see this in action is to look at weight loss. Millions of Americans struggle to lose weight. There are over ten thousand different diets, programs, pills, and products that promise to provide the body you want in thirty days or less if you buy into what they are selling. This may work in the short term, but it won't help you keep the weight off. It has been proven that the majority of people who lose weight quickly with one of these methods gain it back. And what's worse, they end up weighing even more than when they started. That's because no one, including me, wants to eat less and exercise more.

For most people who don't have a health condition that causes weight issues, the solution is basic: eat healthy foods, watch portions, and exercise more. But that advice doesn't sound fun. It isn't sexy. It doesn't come with a money-back guarantee. And it certainly doesn't happen in twenty-one days.

It's the same with finances. Just spend less than you earn. No one wants to hear that either. They want a magic solution that allows them to eat out, go shopping, travel, drive a luxury car, and somehow afford all of that on $50,000 per year.

Self-discipline makes you face reality. It isn't fun. It isn't fast. But it is essential if you're going to get where you want to go. If you want to achieve lasting change and reach your biggest goals, you'll have to get a plan in place, put your head down, and do the work. No matter what your goal is, you will have to dig deep and find it within yourself to say no to the temptations that will try to knock you off your path.

How Do You Stay Motivated?

There are many tips and tricks I can offer to help you keep your motivation strong, but none of them are foolproof. You will still feel unmotivated, and you will still struggle with your self-discipline. It is just part of being human.

When I was a kid, my mom and I would clean the house on Saturday mornings. No one wants to clean the whole house, especially on the weekend. But to make it fun, we would pick out a stack of records. (Yes, I'm that old. Real, vinyl records on a record player.) We would stack them up and drop the needle to start the music playing. Then we would each start our respective chore list for the day and dance, sing, and have fun while we did it.

I still use this trick when I need to get pumped up to work on a big project. I put on whatever Pandora station I am in the mood for, blast that music, and get to work. I have fun planning, organizing, writing, or whatever large task I need to tackle.

How You Do Anything

A business owner I worked with used to say this phrase all the time, and it hits home with me because I value excellence so highly:

"How you do anything is how you do everything."

The origin of this quote is unknown, but some attribute it to Zen Buddhism. Think about this quote and how it relates to your life.

How do you show up for the day?

How do you perform a task when you are in a hurry?

How do you treat another person when you are having a bad day?

This phrase often goes through my mind when I'm rushing through a certain task instead of giving it my full attention and completing it correctly and thoroughly. I stop and think, *If I am slamming this thing together haphazardly, is that how I am going to treat other tasks and projects? Is that how I want to show up for myself and my clients?*

I want things done right. I especially want them done right the first time. I move fast—sometimes too fast—and I must remind myself to slow down and do it right. Not with perfection but with accuracy. You will save so much time and money if you take the time to make a wise decision and complete a project or task correctly. It's better than having to backtrack and fix it later.

This concept comes up a lot when I am working with my coaching and consulting clients. As entrepreneurs, we often fly by the seat of our pants instead of planning out a structured way to do something. In other words, we don't create a system or process. When clients take my course or hire me for consulting, I make them slow down, examine each system and process in their business, and create a standard operating procedure (or SOP). Not one of them is excited to do this work, but I insist upon it—not because I like to torture people but because I know that on the other side of this somewhat daunting process is efficiency, excellence, and freedom.

When you thoroughly plan out a system in your business or life, you start by looking at the processes that make up that system and the tiny steps that make up that process. Ask yourself, "Is this the best way to perform this task? Is this the most efficient way to get the result I want? Do my customers feel like I am providing them with a quality product or service?"

If you want to be successful in life and business, the answers to these questions are critical. Investing the time needed to create smooth and efficient standard operating procedures helps your clients know they are in great hands. They'll be confident that they hired the right person or company for the job, and it cuts down on mistakes. Removing the guesswork and eliminating the constant need to recreate the wheel ensures that you deliver the same quality every time and gives you and your team an easy way to accomplish your goals.

So ponder that statement in your business and your life. How you do anything is how you do everything. And if you know you could be doing things at a higher level, invest the time into creating quality systems and processes.

The Hare and the Tortoise

Aesop's Fables

We all know the famous Aesop Fable called "The Hare and the Tortoise"[24] (although I always thought it was called "The Tortoise and the Hare" until I wrote this chapter). I'm sure the lesson behind this fable is not popular in America, much like delayed gratification is a thing of the past in our current culture. But popular or not, it is time tested and true.

> A Hare was making fun of the Tortoise one day for being so slow.
>
> "Do you ever get anywhere?" he asked with a mocking laugh.
>
> "Yes," replied the Tortoise, "and I get there sooner than you think. I'll run you a race and prove it."
>
> The Hare was much amused at the idea of running a race with the Tortoise, but for the fun of the thing, he agreed. So the Fox, who had consented to act as judge, marked the distance and started the runners off.
>
> The Hare was soon far out of sight, and to make the Tortoise feel very deeply how ridiculous it was for him to try and race with a Hare, he lay down beside the course to take a nap until the Tortoise should catch up.

---

24. The Æsop for Children, "The Hare & the Tortoise," short story presented by Library of Congress, read.gov, accessed May 16, 2024, http://read.gov/aesop/025.html.

The Tortoise meanwhile kept going slowly but steadily, and, after a time, passed the place where the Hare was sleeping. But the Hare slept on very peacefully; and when at last he did wake up, the Tortoise was near the goal. The Hare now ran his swiftest, but he could not overtake the Tortoise in time.

My husband and I got into real estate in 2003. We both sold our respective houses and bought our new house to live in as a married couple. A couple years later, we purchased our first new build to flip. We made enough money from that transaction to remodel the pool at our new home. We purchased our first property to remodel and flip in 2007. The market tanked a week after I listed it for sale, and it has been one of our rental properties ever since. We purchased several other rental properties over the years and put a lot of sweat, blood, and tears into each one. We chose to delay remodeling our own home because every dollar we had went into the rental business. We waited thirteen years before we saved enough to remodel our own house.

We diligently worked and sacrificed and were patient for so long because we knew that slow and steady wins the race. It is not the sexy way to run a business. It is not flashy or Instagram-worthy at all. It is ugly, tedious, difficult, and definitely not fun. But let me tell you, it is so worth it. We live by a very different set of rules than pretty much anyone we know. We don't have nine-to-five jobs, we don't have 401(k)s or pensions, we don't even have employer-paid health care coverage. We push ourselves harder than a boss ever could, and we live life to the fullest in a way only we can. What works for us may not work for someone else. That is where I find my truest rewards.

Every now and then, I lean into my husband and whisper, "I love our life!" I really do. The ups and downs and the slow, long racecourse. I am the tortoise. I have fully embraced it. And at the end of my life, I'll leave a legacy that was built on years of my sweat equity and self-discipline. That is something I can be proud of.

If you are struggling with self-discipline, here is a step-by-step method that has worked well for me:

Step 1

The first step to self-discipline is getting real about where you are right now. Not where you'd like to be, not where your goal sheet says you'll be, but right now. Are you overweight? Get on the scale and write down the actual number. Are you in debt? Add it all up and write the big, scary number down on a piece of paper. You can't possibly change if you don't know where you are starting from.

Step 2

Now that you know, look back on your goal sheet and see where you want to go. Then work through the formula for breaking the goal down into bite-size pieces. You'll have your monthly goals, weekly goals, and daily goals. Get these on your calendar and tape them to the wall.

Step 3

Treat your calendar like it is sacred because your time and goals are valuable. If you don't guard them and treat them with the importance they carry, no one else will. Then faithfully follow your calendar and daily to-do lists. No one else will try as hard as you will to create the life you want. Only you can accomplish this.

Step 4

When you have a setback, get right back up and waste no time worrying about it. Just make the next right move and get back on track immediately.

Step 5

Reward yourself. Give yourself a treat or reward for mini milestones accomplished. You will be amazed at how well this works. If it works for puppies and babies, why wouldn't it work for us?

Here are a few tips and tricks I use for self-discipline.

Make lists: You know by now that my favorite self-discipline tool is my day planner. I use my handwritten task list in combination with my digital calendar. This one is tangible and visual.

Use a habit tracker: I'm a strong believer in visual cues as a form of motivation. There are many different apps and tools available, and I included a PDF with ideas in your book resources.

As a little child, when my mom taught me how to brush my teeth, take a bath, and clean my room regularly, she created a star chart. Every time I completed one of the daily tasks on my chart, I got to pick out a gold, red, blue, or silver star and stick it onto the chart. I loved seeing the colorful stars all over my chart, which showed everything I had accomplished. It made me feel proud, and it motivated me to do more and keep going.

You can invent your own version of a star chart for anything you want to accomplish. Use stickers, markers, or anything fun to mark off your success as you go. Or use one of the habit tracker tools if you prefer. You get to discover what works best for you.

Find an accountability partner: My strongest tool for self-discipline is an accountability partner. I meet with a group of women every Monday via Zoom, and we go over our business goals together. Before we leave the meeting, we share our accountability list for the week. Then we text each other with updates on our progress. It is a great way to build relationships with other achievers and get support to reach your goals. I always build accountability partners into my group coaching programs for this reason.

The key with any hack or trick is to find the one or two that resonate with you the most. I understand that some of the tools I love don't work for some people. We are all wired differently, and that is why there are so many different coaches, mentors, teachers, books, classes, and tools out there. This isn't a one-size-fits-all world, and neither is the path to your personal growth. It has taken me over twenty years and countless hours of reading, researching, learning, and growing to pull together these concepts and ideas. I hope you gain one or two new insights from this book that help you on your journey.

Just Keep Going

When all else fails, just keep going. At the end of the day, if there is one more thing on your to-do list that won't take too long or interfere with going to bed on time, just do it. Finish the last task, cross it off, and go to sleep knowing you didn't give up.

Self-discipline is a skill you can develop. When your mindset, values, and purpose are aligned, sustaining your goals and habits becomes easier. Optimizing your health, finances, and productivity helps self-discipline come more naturally. Redesigning your life for success takes time. But the effort is well worth it.

Books That Changed My Life

The War of Art: Break through the Blocks and Win Your Inner Creative Battles by Steven Pressfield

The Compound Effect: Multiply Your Success One Simple Step at a Time by Darren Hardy

Chapter 10 Action Steps and Resources

Self-discipline worksheet

Chapter 11

Resilience

resilience: *noun*

"an ability to recover from or adjust easily to misfortune or change"[25]

Or phrased another way, "The capacity to recover quickly from difficulties; toughness."

When life kicks you down, you don't just get to lie there and cry. You might lie there for a minute until you think, "It's okay. I'll figure it out." And then you have to get back up and keep moving forward.

Hardships Sharpen Your Resilience

Let's pretend. You were born into a perfect, loving family. You are beautiful, smart, and talented. Everything comes easy to you. You wish for something, and there it is—no effort required. You've never known struggle, hardship, or pain. Life is perfect, and so are you.

---

25. "resilience,"*Merriam-Webster Dictionary*, merriam-webster.com, accessed May 16, 2024, https://www.merriam-webster.com/dictionary/resilience.

A dream we sometimes wish for, right? But it is actually a great tragedy.

Struggle makes you stronger. When you never struggle, when you never reach for something, when you never have to try, you miss out on strengthening your character. You lose the opportunity to sharpen and grow your inner strength. You don't fully become who you were meant to be. Hardship makes us tough. We fall down, and then we have to figure out how to get back up. We have to learn lessons the hard way many times because sometimes, that is the only way to rise up and become someone greater than we ever imagined.

When walking through the story of my life, I can see how resilience shaped me into the person I am today.

I was about six when my parents split up. They separated for almost two years before finally making the divorce official. It was decided that I would live with my mom and visit my dad on certain weekends. I remember moving into a low-end mobile home. If you've never heard of a HUD home, this was one of those. A tiny tin single-wide on a dirt lot in Phoenix. It was all we could afford, but at least Mom and I had a place of our own.

I put huge pressure on myself to do well in school, earn good grades, and be a good kid. I always did my chores and my homework without being asked. I kept my room clean and did what I was told. I became very self-sufficient. I distinctly remember telling my mom that I realized I couldn't count on anyone else, so I would just have to take care of myself. I was eight years old.

When I graduated high school, I earned a scholarship to the Rocky Mountain College of Art & Design in Denver. My dream was to attend art school. Having never lived anywhere but Phoenix, driving to a new town to live with three roommates and start a new life all by myself was a big adjustment. As an only child, it was tough. I made a ton of mistakes and still wish I'd done things differently.

One of the hardest experiences was dropping out of art school after my grants were taken away. Being punished for working while putting myself through college seemed so unfair. I drove back to Phoenix from Denver and cried the whole way. I hated giving up my dream.

Never in a million years did I think I'd get into real estate. It fell into my lap and changed the trajectory of my life in a way I would have never imagined. And if real estate was a surprise twist, becoming a landlord was even more of a shock. If there is one thing that has given me resilience (and a ton of gray hair), it is owning rental properties.

These are just a few of the moments in my young life that shaped me into the person I am today. These experiences left an indelible mark on my personality and gave me the strength to become an entrepreneur, take risks, handle rejection, and push through when I didn't think I could continue on.

I've had to make ten thousand pivots. From family changes to school changes. From lifelong career goals to too many different jobs. From being an artist to becoming a real estate investor. I've learned to embrace change and welcome it as an old friend.

What Makes Some People Keep on Trying and Some People Give Up?

I have heard the answer to this question many times through books, podcasts, seminars, and workshops. They call it your "why."

What is your why? Why do you get out of bed in the morning? For your spouse? For your children? For your career? Your why is your passion, your purpose, your reason for pushing through difficulty. Your motivation for getting back up after you've been knocked down again.

John Maxwell said, "When you find your why, you find your way."[26]

Your why has to have weight. It can't just be "I get out of bed every morning to make money."

Money is indeed a motivator because we have bills and needs we have to pay for. But money is not a compelling reason.

I am an artist. God has given me a great gift and a privilege. Even when I don't feel inspired or excited by painting, I still feel a deep need to create. When I've received my fiftieth rejection letter or a hurtful comment about my work from a stranger—or worse, a friend—I still somehow go back into the studio and do it all again. Fulfilling this gift is one of my biggest whys.

I am also a lifelong entrepreneur. I am wired differently than others. I love to brainstorm new business ideas. I love to build things from

---

26. Servant Leadership Institute, "John Maxwell: Find Your Why," YouTube.com, August 22, 2013, https://www.youtube.com/watch?v=lkf217c_b3M.

nothing. I need to walk my own road. And now I get to help others pursue their dreams—and that is one of the greatest whys I have ever had.

Why does having a why matter?

Here's the truth. Even the most driven, self-motivated, disciplined people get tired of trying all the time. Even the most self-controlled people tire of doing the unfun parts of life. When success eludes them for the thousandth time, even the strongest person may want to give up. When you have a true reason deep in your heart for getting out of bed, for trying again, for putting yourself out there, it will get you through the hard times when you just don't think you can continue on.

Have you gone through struggles? Have you experienced hardships? How have you tapped into that resiliency you needed to keep pushing through? I'll share a few of my experiences and tools that have helped me tap into the courage I've needed to be resilient.

Say Yes to Things You've Never Done Before

In 2012, I started researching and reading books about building an art business. I would go to the Scottsdale Art Walk on Thursday nights and visit galleries. I met a gallery owner and artist who chatted with me about my desire to pursue art as a business. She told me the first step was to join a local art league. She said I'd make some good connections and start by doing my first shows. This would give me practice and exposure. I'm so grateful for the time she gave me that night.

I went home and researched local art leagues. I discovered that The Scottsdale Artists League met once a month, very near my house. One night, I signed up at the front table, then sat down and listened to the president speak about all the news and happenings in the league. They were passing out sign-up sheets for their best show of the year. It was a paint-out (where artists paint outdoors) at the Desert Botanical Garden. For four weekends, the artists would paint on-site in the garden. On the final weekend, they would have a big show to sell the finished paintings. Everyone had to volunteer for a different task, and we gave a small percentage of our proceeds to the league.

I was sitting at a table with a few other artists when the sign-up sheets were passed out. I started filling in my information right away. A lady leaned over to me and asked, "Have you ever done an art show before?" I said no. She asked, "Have you ever painted outside before?" I said no. Then she asked, "And you just signed up for this event?" I said yes.

I'm sure this woman thought it was crazy that I had just dived right in and said yes, even though I'd never done these things. However, I have learned that this is an incredible key to pursuing your dreams. When you don't know what you are doing but do know that it is leading you in the direction you want to go, dive in and say yes.

I had fun painting for those four weekends in the garden. I created some beautiful watercolor paintings. And I learned a ton of new things about creating, marketing, and selling art. I matted, framed, and priced my artwork. And on the weekend of the big sale, I sold every single one.

In 2023, I was starting my coaching and consulting business. I reached out to an amazing friend who is the vice president of a title company, and we met for lunch. I shared my news about my new business with her, and, being the awesome woman she is, she immediately offered to help. She said she was hosting an educational event in four weeks that I should plan on attending. She suggested I make flyers about my business to hand out to everyone and prepare a five-minute presentation on my coaching offer.

Inside, I was scared to death. I don't usually stand up and speak in front of people. But I knew this would be a pivotal moment in launching my business. Without hesitation, I said yes.

Now that my business is growing and thriving, I'm so glad I did!

Overcome the Fear

When I was a senior in high school, I got a job at the mall. It was one of those accessory stores that sell costume jewelry, hair ties, purses, and all the fun things teenage girls love! My many duties at the store included running the cash register, doing inventory, selling products, providing customer service, and piercing people's ears. I was quite a bit nervous about this last part of my new job and kind of avoided it for the first month or so. All I could think was, *What if I miss? What if I hit a nerve? What if they cry, scream, or yell? What if I paralyze them for life?*

When my manager taught me how to pierce ears, she took a giant stuffed teddy bear, loaded an earring into the ear-piercing gun, and shot it into the bear's ear. All is well and good for a stuffed animal. There is no flesh or blood or crying. Needless to say, I was still not sure if I could successfully do this on a human customer. All of my fears kept flooding back to me every time someone came in and asked for this service.

I knew there was only one way I could get over this fear.

My ears had been pierced at age eight, but that was too long ago for me to remember what it felt like. One day before work, I went in early. I disinfected my ear in the new earring location. I used the gun, and whammo, I pierced my own ear. There was a loud click, a quick pinch, and a little bit of a burning sensation, but that was it. I didn't miss, I didn't scream, I didn't cry. I did it! I successfully pierced a human's flesh, and it was my own, so I knew exactly how it felt!

This experience cured my fear and gave me so much confidence. When my first customer came in that day to get their ear pierced, I stepped right up and accomplished the task like I had done it a thousand times.

There are certain things—certain fears—that you have to conquer in order to move forward. I couldn't just tell my boss, "Sorry, I don't pierce people." I would have gotten fired. I had to find a way to get past it in order to grow and excel in my new position.

Many of our fears are much like this story. We build so much dread and drama into what might happen. We create a story of pain and fear and what-ifs. But much like piercing my own ear, the reality is usually so much faster and way less fearful. In less than a minute, I solved this thing I'd been building up in my head for weeks. In less than a minute, I was able to move forward.

If we would only face our fears sooner, just think how much time and wasted worry we could avoid.

Give It a Week

I have a funny little theory that has worked for me many, many times. Whenever you are facing something difficult or new and are struggling so hard with it that you think you'll never win or get through it, just give it a week. Seven days. That's how it works.

I started wearing eyeglasses in the seventh grade. Oh, yes, braces, glasses, and straight-A student—that was me. Super popular! I never minded glasses, but when I turned eighteen and was living in Denver to attend art school, I asked my eye doctor about contact lenses. I just imagined how different I would look without glasses and thought about the freedom I would have, being able to wear contacts with cute nonprescription drug store sunglasses. My doctor took measurements and said I was a candidate for disposable soft contact lenses. They showed me how to put them in my eyes in the doctor's office and then sent me home with a few boxes. It seemed easy to put them in and take them out while at the doctor's office.

But when I got up for school the next day and tried to put them on in my bathroom, it was painful and tricky. I couldn't get myself to shove this foreign object into my eye. I kept pulling down my lower eyelid and trying to balance this tiny, watery lens on my finger. But it was awkward, and it hurt. I'm sure I cried. I finally put on my glasses and went to school.

I felt like such a failure and didn't think I would be able to master this task. But I tried again the next day, and the next day, and the next. After one week of pulling, poking, tearing up, and yelling, I finally got it. I mastered this new technique without pain or panic, and I felt so beautiful in my new contact lenses.

A few months after overcoming this little hurdle, I drove down to Phoenix to return my dad's car and pick up a used Nissan pickup truck I'd purchased. It was a stick shift, and I knew how to drive a standard vehicle, but it had been a while. I had never owned one before, but my Uncle Bill had taught me to drive one. After I bought the truck, I had to get right back to Denver for school, so I took off the next day. Driving on the freeways and highways was a breeze, so I was confident that I had made a great purchase and was pleased that driving a stick shift had come back to me so quickly.

That was until the hill.

In Denver, there was a steep hill that I had to climb up and turn left at every day. It was unavoidable, and I never even paid attention to this hill until I had to go up it and wait at an incline for my turn to go left. Every standard vehicle is a bit different, especially cars vs. trucks. This pickup truck was different for me on day one of driving it in the city. I kept sliding backward down the hill and stalling it out. A line of cars stacked up behind me, and the drivers were furious. They were honking, yelling, and, I'm sure, swearing angrily. I had made them miss the left-turn arrow three times! I was crying hysterically. There was no way to get out of this situation except to keep trying.

Finally, I made it up the hill and through the light, but I was terrified to go on any more hills. I seriously thought that buying the truck was a huge mistake and wondered if I could sell it or give it back. But the next day, I woke up and knew I had to keep pressing forward. I couldn't just avoid all the hills forever. I kept driving each day, trying to improve and get a feel for this particular truck's clutch and shifting patterns. After one week of screaming, yelling, cursing, and crying, I got it. I mastered driving that little Nissan truck, and I drove it for over ten years.

Now, I know my one-week plan will not work for all of life's problems, but many times, it does. If I get a cold, instead of getting upset and freaking out about all the things I will miss or get behind on, I take a deep breath and remind myself to give it a week. I will feel better then, and everything will be okay. When I'm trying to learn a new software program or skill, I try to be patient with myself and just give it a week. I know I'll have learned more and become familiar with how to do it in seven days.

I promise it helps me a lot. And I hope it will help you the next time you face something you think you can't do or conquer.

Failure

I was talking with an artist friend and shared my story about what I'd gone through over the years with my art career. I'd started out brave and eager and excited for all that lay ahead of me. I embraced each new opportunity and gave it my all. And I had success. I was getting into shows, winning awards, and selling art. Each year was better than the last. I played a game with myself to see if I could double my art sales every year. And it actually happened for the first four years.

In 2016, my dreams came true. I got into a prestigious Scottsdale art gallery! This is what so many artists want. The night I pulled up to the gallery for my very first solo art show, I sat in my car and welled up with tears of joy when I saw all my paintings hanging on the walls.

I'd made it! I had arrived. All of my family and friends came to my show. Everyone was so proud and so supportive. It was a night I'll never forget.

But the next two years were a struggle. Sales were definitely not where I needed them to be. Then, in 2018, my beloved gallery closed down permanently. It was not a shock because so many galleries were closing their doors, but it still hurt. I was crushed. In 2019, my sales went down to nothing, and in 2020, with the pandemic, it wasn't much better.

I finally had to make peace with myself and ask why I was creating art. Was it for money, or was it because I was given this incredible gift that I love and want to share with the world? After many self-talk sessions like this one, I started creating art for myself, not for the hope of a sale and not for anyone else's preference. I started painting intuitively, using a more abstract technique that many people didn't understand or like.

By 2023, I had created almost forty new paintings and had the biggest solo show of my art career. It was a huge success, and I could tell this new work resonated with others because my show was nearly sold out by the end.

I'm so glad I listened to my intuition and followed my inner vision for the direction of my art career. If I had stopped creating when the business appeared to be failing, I never would have experienced the success of that show and the connections made between all my new collectors and my new artwork.

Reframing Failure

Tom Bilyeu said, "Past failures can only haunt you if you think they define who you are today. It's only when you run from the lesson or wish you were perfect that you're haunted by your past. Reframe your past as your education. Learn and move on."[27]

He loves Tony Robbins's question: Look at the worst thing that's ever happened to you and ask "How is this the best thing that's ever happened to me?" By interrupting your negative thought pattern that assumes only bad comes from an event in your life, you can reframe it as a growth opportunity by asking yourself these expansive questions that lead to your upward trajectory:

- What could I have done differently?
- What skills could I develop that would have helped me in this situation?
- What lesson do I choose to learn from this failure?

27.Tom Bilyeu (@TomBilyeu), "Past failures can only haunt you if you think they define who you are.today..., Twitter post, twitter.com, March 31, 2019, https://x.com/TomBilyeu/status/1112370465681616896

Now, your mind is focused on positivity and growth, not shame and regret. Reframing your past helps you move forward and become better as a result.[28]

Write Your Own Definition of Success

What does success look like to you? You will need to dig deep for this one because it is too easy to define what success looks like for our culture, our world, our friends, or even our family. But their definitions do not matter. What makes you feel successful? What is the definition of success that lights you up inside? If you were to write out your own personal description of what a successful life means to you, what would that be?

Others' definitions of success often do not align with our own. For example, when I tell people that I am an artist, nine times out of ten, their response is, "Are you in a gallery?" For the average person in America who doesn't create art for a living, this is the perceived mark of success. If the answer is yes, they seem inquisitive and impressed, and they want to know more about what I do. If the answer is no, they act dismissive and uncomfortable with the conversation. I have learned over many years that this is not an insult or anyone's fault. Most people just don't understand art or the people who create it.

There is a fantastic book I love called *Still Writing: The Perils and Pleasures of a Creative Life* by Dani Shapiro, who writes about her

---

28. Impact Theory (homepage), impacttheory.com, accessed May 16, 2024, https://impacttheory.com/blog/ask-these-questions-to-reframe-your-perspective-on-life/.

friend Mark, a very prominent sculptor. In the book, Mark pulls Dani aside at a dinner party:

> "Somebody just asked me if I was still doing my sculpture thing," he said.
>
> I laughed.
>
> "I'm serious," he said. "How was I supposed to respond? 'Are you still doing that brain surgery thing?'"

Dani goes on to note how many times she has been asked if she is still writing and ends the book with this beautiful prose:

> Still writing? I usually nod and smile, then quickly change the subject. But here is what I would like to put down my fork and say: "Yes, yes, I am. I will write until the day I die, or until I am robbed of my capacity to reason. Even if my fingers were to clench and wither, even if I were to grow deaf or blind, even if I were unable to move a muscle in my body save for the blink of one eye, I would still write."[29]

Anyone pursuing a dream can relate to this careless question disguised as small talk at a party. You don't have to be an artist or a writer to feel the knife cut through your identity and passion as someone asks if you are still doing the thing you love. The thing you've sacrificed such long hours for. The thing you've given yourself over to that is your body, mind, and soul.

---

29. Dani Shaprio, *Still Writing: The Perils and Pleasures of a Creative Life* (New York, NY: Grove Press, 2014).

But that is where resilience comes in. It gives you the power to smile and nod at that person's simple question, say, "Yes," and then move on because they will never get what your dream means to you. They will never understand what it takes to get back up after you've been knocked down a hundred times. They don't understand. And that's okay. Because there is a community of dreamers, artists, and entrepreneurs like you and me who get it. We are here for each other, and we will never ask, "Still writing?"

The Hits Keep Coming

Resilience sounds great when you read it on the page or when someone posts a quote about it on social media. But what do you do on the days when everything in the world seems to be going wrong? When one thing after the other just keeps knocking you down? I think these days test our resilience more than any other time in our lives. It doesn't take much resilience to enjoy a good day. It doesn't even take much when one big problem occurs because we usually drop everything else and focus on resolving the issue as quickly as possible. My patience and strength are stretched to the max when I have too many things screwing up all at once. That is when I lose it.

I'm hoping I'm not the only one. I'm hoping you can relate. I wish I had a magical solution that made days like these far and few between, but I don't.

Here are a few tips and tricks that seem to get me through:

- I write on a piece of paper everything that is stressing me out. It helps to get it all out there, no matter how ugly it all is.

- I do some deep breathing, prayer, or meditation, or I just sit in silence to calm myself down.

- I go for walks or bike rides. Moving my body and being in nature are two fast-working cures that help get my mind right again.

- I put on some great music—something happy and upbeat to get my feet tapping and my face smiling again. It is important to find ways to feel good, even when your day is going sideways.

- Once I am feeling better, I am ready to put things into perspective. I count my blessings, I practice gratitude, and if I need a new perspective on how small my problems are on this day, I remind myself that I don't have a terminal illness, I don't live in extreme poverty, I don't have to dig ditches in 110-degree heat. Extremes like this, which are a reality for others, help me remember that I have an amazing life and will get through all the problems and frustrations listed on my piece of paper.

A few other tricks that can help you on days like this are reading a motivational book, listening to an inspiring podcast, calling an encouraging friend, or treating yourself to something nice, like a special coffee drink, a new magazine, a manicure, or anything that makes you feel good.

Resilience is about getting through and pulling yourself back up when you feel like lying down and giving up—especially when you feel like you are doing everything alone as an entrepreneur. Especially in real estate, when the market shifts overnight and it feels like you are starting all over again. Especially as a creative, when you feel like you are pouring your heart and soul into your work but just can't seem to get the sales you need to survive.

When you get through a tough day or a difficult stage and can look back at the you then and the you now, knowing that you chose strength, courage, and resilience will grow your confidence like nothing else can.

Books That Changed My Life

The Alchemist by Paulo Coelho

Excuses Begone: How to Change Lifelong, Self-Defeating Thinking Habits by Dr. Wayne Dyer

Grit: The Power of Passion and Perseverance by Angela Duckworth

Chapter 11 Action Steps and Resources

Overcomer worksheet

Chapter 12
Essential

What does it mean to live an essential life? In a world overflowing with distractions, obligations, and endless pursuits, finding what is truly essential can feel like a monumental task. Yet, the power of clarity lies in distilling your life down to what is most important. To live essentially is to strip away the non-essentials, to focus on what truly matters, and to align every decision, action, and thought with your core values and deepest desires. This chapter is about cutting through the noise and zeroing in on the essence of what makes life meaningful and fulfilling.

What is *essential*?

Merriam-Webster defines *essential* as:

1: extremely important and necessary

2: very basic : FUNDAMENTAL

When you ask most people what is important to them or what their priorities are, they will give you a long list—family, career, fitness, sports, friendships, and more. But this response raises an important question: *If ALL of these things are top priorities, is anything truly important?* The word *priority* is singular, meaning the most important thing. Much like the definition of *essential.* What is extremely important? What is necessary? What matters the most to you?

Once you define this for yourself, you will need to learn to let the rest of the list move down in the hierarchy. As author Greg McKeown says in his book *Essentialism: The Disciplined Pursuit of Less*, you must learn "the disciplined pursuit of less."

Throughout this book, we've explored the significance of mindset, purpose, goals, habits, and more in shaping a fulfilling life and achieving meaningful success. Each of these concepts acts as a compass, guiding you toward what truly matters. Your mindset shapes your perspective, empowering you to see opportunities where others see obstacles. Your values serve as guideposts along your path. Your purpose gives you direction, anchoring your decisions in deeper meaning. Goals provide milestones, marking your progress toward your aspirations. Habits establish the daily rituals that reinforce your values and propel you toward your vision of success. Optimizing your health and finances serves as a holistic anchor supporting your journey. Effective time management ensures that you approach each day with efficiency and productivity, while self-discipline and resilience maintain your focus and determination.

So, how do you discover what is essential in your life?

Here are a few simple practices that have helped me focus on what is essential and bring me back to an intentional space where I can achieve great things.

Simplify

I have a deep desire for simplicity. I know this desire is not unique to me. Many people are exhausted, stressed, frazzled, stretched too thin, and feeling pressure from all sides. When did we allow our lives to get so out of control? When did we fill our homes with so much stuff that we have to pay monthly fees at self-storage units? When did we cram our garages so full of possessions that we can't park a car in them? When did we pack our calendars so full of obligations that we don't have time for our family or best friends? When did we overload our minds with tasks, anxieties, and expectations so much so that we can't sit peacefully in a room and just be still?

If you want to create the life of your dreams, discover your purpose, set extraordinary goals, and live a life you desire, it will require that you do things differently.

It may be time to ruthlessly eliminate the excess of possessions, activities, negative thought patterns, and unrealistic expectations and get back to basics. Because life is short. If we are not finding joy in our professions, our relationships, and ourselves, then something is wrong.

Schedule

Is your schedule so full that you can't find time to rest?

I look at my day planner as an effective litmus test. I schedule my top tasks of the day based on my overarching goal. It could be my goal for the week, the month, or my life. As I work toward the goal that matters the most to me and the time it will take to reach that goal, I have to make certain decisions. There will be things I have to say no to. There will be people I have to say no to. As amazing as I like to think I am, I can't do it all. So, if a request doesn't fit into my schedule, which I must keep in order to reach my greatest goals, I will have to politely decline.

Will people be disappointed? Yes, they might.

But if you are trying to achieve great things with the one life you've been given, you'll have to make choices. You will have to choose what is most important over what is easy.

Be Present

In an age when technology connects us more than ever, people are experiencing the highest rates of depression, anxiety, loneliness, and feelings of separation, leading to mental health issues and even suicide. The digital world infiltrates every aspect of modern life, creating a barrier between people despite being able to "connect" 24/7.

Look at any busy restaurant, and you'll see couples, families, and friends, all heads down, staring at phones rather than looking into one another's eyes. Where is the true eye-to-eye connection? The joy of feeling understood and connected?

A few years ago, I started a little trick with my husband to improve our date nights. When we go out for a special evening, I leave my phone at home. This change made our evenings so much better! Before, I would get business-related calls or texts at dinner, distracting me and pulling me away from our time together. Now, I am 100 percent focused on being present, more attentive, and engaged with him. This shift has enriched our relationship immensely.

Surround Yourself with Beauty

Add things to your home that are beautiful and bring you joy. A mason jar with freshly picked wildflowers. Or a vase with roses from the store. A candle that smells like vanilla cookies. A hand-painted work of art from a local artist. A green houseplant in a colorful pot. A freshly baked loaf of bread. A framed photo of your family or best friend. Whatever you find visually appealing or helpful in creating a sense of home or luxury for you, add it to your home or office. Surrounding yourself with beauty elevates your mood and helps you appreciate the things you are grateful for.

The Way Forward

In this book, you have delved into the depths of mindset, values, true purpose, goal setting, habits, health, finances, time management, self-discipline, resilience, and what is essential in designing success on your own terms. I've crafted each concept, strategy, and story I've shared with you to illuminate your path, empower your decisions, and ignite the flame of possibility within you.

As you reflect on the pages you've turned and the insights you've gained, remember that this is not merely a collection of words but a road map to transformation. Please embrace these lessons not as simple theories but as actionable steps toward designing a life and business that resonate with your deepest desires and aspirations. I'll be thrilled if you take just a handful of actionable items from this book and embed them into your daily routine until they become second nature. Witnessing those small changes grow into transformative habits is where the real magic happens.

I've emphasized the importance of authenticity and alignment. Your journey is uniquely yours, and what works for someone else may not necessarily be the right fit for you. So, I encourage you to approach these principles with an open mind and choose those that connect most with your values and vision.

Being an entrepreneur or high achiever is the more difficult path. It can feel lonely, scary, and overwhelming. There will be moments of doubt, setbacks, and challenges along the way. But in the midst of all that, there's a beauty—a sense of fulfillment that comes from pursuing your passion and carving out your own path in this world. And if it is your life's calling, you won't ever want to let that go.

I hope my stories and strategies have resonated with you, providing practical guidance that you can seamlessly weave into your daily life or business operations. They are not meant to be complicated additions but rather helpful tools that streamline and simplify, ultimately leading you toward the time freedom and financial freedom you've been searching for.

You have within you the power to create the life and business of your dreams. My goal is that you will go forward with confidence, knowing you possess the wisdom, strength, and determination to turn your aspirations into reality.

Thank you for allowing me to be a part of your journey. Here's to your continued success, growth, and fulfillment. Know that my support and encouragement are with you every step of the way.

Books That Changed My Life

Essentialism: The Disciplined Pursuit of Less by Greg McKeown

Walden: Life in the Woods by Henry David Thoreau

Action Steps and Resources

Use the link below to download all of my book resources for each chapter:

andreamerican.com/redesignbook

Let's Connect!

Congratulations! You learned many new tools and strategies for redesigning your life and creating success on your own terms. Whether you are an entrepreneur, a high achiever, a business owner, or a goal-setting star, these action steps will help you reach the next level you are seeking.

But the journey doesn't end here. Let's connect!

1. Access All Your Free Resources

As a thank-you for reading my book, I have created valuable resources you can use to take action after each chapter.

Visit andreamerican.com/redesignbook to get all the free resources mentioned in this book.

2. Connect on Social Media

I'd love to connect with you on social media. Send me a note to say hi!

You can find me on Instagram at @andrea_merican

3. Ways to Work Together

Are you ready to level up your business and get some support and strategies to maximize your time? Let's see if we are a good fit for business coaching or consulting. Head over to andreamerican.com and explore all the different ways we can work together.

Make a Lasting Impact

Thank you for taking the time to read my book! I hope you found it to be insightful, encouraging, and the next step in designing your own success story.

I would greatly appreciate it if you could leave a review sharing your thoughts and impressions on Amazon or any other platform where you purchased or read the book. Your feedback is invaluable and helps other readers discover the book.

Your support means the world to me, and I'm grateful for your time and consideration.

Acknowledgments

I would like to express my heartfelt gratitude to my husband, Paul, for his unwavering support and encouragement throughout my entrepreneurial journey. Your belief in me and your willingness to champion my goals and ideas have been invaluable beyond measure. Thank you for being my best friend, my sounding board, and my constant source of strength. This book would not have been possible without you.

About the Author

Andrea Merican is an author, artist, business coach, investor, seasoned real estate professional, and world-traveling entrepreneur, embodying a legacy of incredible accomplishments and financial success. But she didn't start out on that path.

Growing up as the only child of a hardworking single mother, Andrea faced financial hardship from a young age. Despite these challenges, she pursued her passion for art and never lost sight of her dreams. After receiving a partial scholarship to art school and starting her first business painting murals, Andrea faced unexpected obstacles that forced her to drop out of college and work retail for minimum wage. But she didn't give up.

She continued to take night classes at community college and eventually landed her first job in property management. That's when she was introduced to computers and began her journey into the world of online business. At age twenty-five, Andrea helped her dad create a successful eBay business grossing one million dollars and, eventually, launched her own online business selling home theater projector screens.

But once again, life threw her a curveball when the market shifted, and her business failed overnight. She pivoted once again, earning her real estate license in a down market, which led to her first experience as a real estate investor. From there, she worked for a real estate investment start-up and became a key member in growing the company to have over fifty employees and bring in millions of dollars in annual revenue.

Eventually, she left the company to focus on her art business, which she'd launched in 2011. She continued to travel the world, paint, win multiple awards, and sell her work. She eventually became instrumental in building another real estate investment start-up, growing to have over twenty employees and agents and bring in millions of dollars in annual revenue.

In 2021, Andrea focused on painting and teaching art classes and took a two-month road trip across the country with her husband. Today, she is fulfilling her long-held dream of business coaching and consulting, sharing her knowledge and experience to help others pursue their passions and fulfill their lifelong dreams too.

Despite facing financial hardship and unexpected setbacks, Andrea is proof that with determination and hard work, anyone can achieve their goals and create their own success story.

www.ingramcontent.com/pod-product-compliance
Lightning Source LLC
Chambersburg PA
CBHW071327120626
46546CB00002B/477